30-MINUTE
WHOLE-FOOD, PLANT-BASED
COOKBOOK

30-MINUTE
WHOLE-FOOD, PLANT-BASED
COOKBOOK

EASY RECIPES WITH NO SALT, OIL, OR REFINED SUGAR

Kathy A. Davis

Photography by Hélène Dujardin

ROCKRIDGE
PRESS

For general information on our other products and services or to obtain technical support, please contact our Customer Care Department within the United States at (866) 744-2665, or outside the United States at (510) 253-0500.

Rockridge Press publishes its books in a variety of electronic and print formats. Some content that appears in print may not be available in electronic books, and vice versa.

TRADEMARKS: Rockridge Press and the Rockridge Press logo are trademarks or registered trademarks of Callisto Media Inc. and/or its affiliates, in the United States and other countries, and may not be used without written permission. All other trademarks are the property of their respective owners. Rockridge Press is not associated with any product or vendor mentioned in this book.

Interior and Cover Designer: Regina Stadnik
Art Producer: Tom Hood
Editor: Justin Hartung
Production Editor: Ashley Polikoff

Photography by Hélène Dujardin © 2020. Food styling by Anna Hampton.

ISBN: Print 978-1-64876-009-9
eBook 978-1-64876-018-1
R0

To my husband, John,
thank you for your support.
To my parents, thank you
for teaching me I can achieve
anything I put my mind to.
I love you all!

Creamy Corn Grits with Kale and Mushrooms, page 29

CONTENTS

INTRODUCTION

My journey with whole-food, plant-based (WFPB) eating started more than six years ago when my husband, John, brought up the idea during a dinner conversation. He had read some contradictory articles about "healthy eating" and started exploring some of the research around the WFPB diet. I remember digging my heels in, saying things like, "I'll try it, but I'm not giving up my cheeseburgers and Buffalo wings." So dramatic!

After experimenting with some plant-based recipes (veggie burgers and Buffalo cauliflower included), I realized this wasn't so bad. In fact, it was delicious. I uncovered stories of other real-life people following a WFPB diet who reversed symptoms of common American diseases such as cancer, heart disease, and diabetes. I knew I was on the right track to sustain a healthy lifestyle with this way of eating. As my journey with the diet continued, I looked into the ethical and environmental reasons that people might follow a meat-free diet. I learned how the diet can affect far more than an individual's health. For example, by not eating meat, you avoid supporting an industry that inflicts cruelty upon animals. Additionally, the water used to raise animals for food far exceeds the amount used to grow plants. And the greenhouse gases that animal agriculture farms produce exceeds the amount generated by the cars we drive. So I started eating vegan, and although it seemed extreme to some of the people in my life, it felt right to me.

Over the years I've tried lots of imitation meat and dairy products and eaten at hundreds of vegan and vegan-friendly restaurants. And I've shared many vegan recipes made with these products on my website, VegInspired.com. Although I enjoyed plenty of these foods, I was always drawn toward a WFPB diet, which is similar to a vegan way of eating but with a focus on dishes made only with whole-food ingredients.

It was in November 2019 that I made a complete switch to WFPB. That month, I stepped on the scale and saw that I was at my heaviest weight ever. With a history of heart disease, diabetes, and cancer in my family, I knew that being overweight increased my chances of disease, regardless of the "healthy" vegan diet I followed at the time (many store-bought cookies might be vegan, but they are not healthy). So I started rereading *The Starch Solution* by John McDougall and *How Not to Die* by Michael Greger. I talked to my husband, John, about sticking to a WFPB diet specifically for weight loss. He agreed. We hit the grocery store armed with a list of WFPB ingredients and a meal plan focused on healthy starches and lots of vegetables.

After six months of eating WFPB meals, we had each lost more than 30 pounds. I am wearing jeans and shirt sizes I haven't worn in more than a decade. Eating this way—and making sure I'm getting regular exercise (I track how many steps I get in a day)—has changed my life. I wasn't surprised that I lost weight on the diet; rather, I was surprised by how good I felt. Since day one, I've felt lighter and more energized. A WFPB diet has helped me with acid reflux, reduced joint pain from years of cheerleading, and even cleared up my adult acne. By increasing my water intake and eating more fiber, my digestive system works more efficiently, too. The benefits of this way of eating are almost immeasurable.

And it's delicious, too. By focusing on whole foods, you learn to enjoy the natural flavors and textures of food more. Whether you're brand new to plant-based eating, a vegan or vegetarian looking to follow a stricter WFPB diet, or someone who has been eating WFPB for some time, I am here to guide you. The 30-minute recipes in this book are simple and will make eating healthfully easy for you, regardless of where you are on your journey.

CHAPTER 1

WHOLE-FOOD, PLANT-BASED MADE EASY

I am thrilled to have you join me in making easy and tasty whole-food, plant-based (WFPB) recipes in just 30 minutes or less. I have seen tremendous health and wellness benefits from eating this way, and I hope that you enjoy this collection of some of my favorite recipes. Whether you picked up this book out of curiosity about the WFPB movement or you wish to add more quick plant-based meals to your repertoire, these recipes will make sticking to this healthy and delicious way of eating as stress-free as possible. In this chapter, you'll learn about the principles of a WFPB diet, what you can expect from the recipes, and tips and tricks to help you meet your healthy-eating goals.

WFPB FAST FACTS

The term "whole-food, plant-based" has found its way into mainstream conversation. And yet there is still some confusion over its exact meaning. For this book's purposes, it means the recipes contain only nonprocessed or minimally processed ingredients that come from plants and use little to no added salt, oil, or refined sugar. But don't think that means bland food: the vegetables, fruits, beans, and whole grains used in these recipes are jam-packed with flavor.

Eating a WFPB diet along with exercising regularly is an optimum way to achieve a healthy lifestyle. Note that although the term "diet" comes up a lot in this book, it is in reference to a manner of eating, not a short-term meal plan or typical weight-loss diet. WFPB eating is not about counting calories or foods; rather, it is about incorporating whole-food, plant-based ingredients into your meals and habits.

The Power of Plants

Plant-based foods are foods derived from plants in their most complete form. Packed with nutrients, a plant-based diet consisting of a variety of foods can satisfy all of your nutritional needs. Plant-based diets provide an increase in soluble fiber, which is extremely important for your digestive system and gut bacteria. Most Americans eat significantly less than the recommended daily amount of fiber, which is around 25 to 30 grams per day. Eating a variety of plant-based foods (beans, grains, fruits, and vegetables) allows you to get your daily recommended values of fiber, protein, calcium, and healthy fats.

Perhaps you shouldn't be surprised to learn animal-based foods are not a component of a WFPB diet. These include meats, fish, poultry, eggs, cheeses, milk, and other dairy products, as well as any other foods containing animal products such as whey, lactose, and rennet. Many animal-based foods have a high amount of cholesterol and saturated fat that can be harmful to our bodies, especially our cardiovascular and organ systems.

Before I had learned about the WFPB diet, I would say things like "Yes, heart disease runs in my family." But I didn't realize that one of the causes was the way my family ate. I grew up on the Standard American Diet, which doesn't adhere to whole-food or plant-based principles. When I started eating WFPB, I was worried I wouldn't be able to enjoy the same dishes I grew up with. However, as I began to craft recipes, I realized I could re-create the same flavors and textures of my favorite dishes without using any animal products. As more and more people adopt a WFPB lifestyle, we'll be able to reverse and prevent many of our common American diseases by diet alone. I've met plant-based eaters who believe that the diet helped reduce their heart disease, diabetes, and even cancer symptoms. The bottom line: I believe in the power of plants to help you live a healthy life.

The Whole (Food) Story

Whole foods are foods that are unrefined with no (or minimal) processing. They are healthy for you because they still possess their nutritional components and provide necessary nutrients, vitamins, and minerals for vitality and longevity. Plant-based ingredients left in their complete form give us the "good stuff," because processing can strip away the essential nutrients. Foods are typically processed to increase their shelf life or to satisfy a popular nutritional claim like "low fat." When buying something that is seemingly whole food, like chili powder or lime juice, I encourage you to read the ingredients to be sure there are no unpronounceable preservatives or other problematic ingredients such as the lime oil in lime juice or soybean oil in chili powder. That is a sure sign that the product is not a whole food. Processed foods pose a problem since they often contain a large amount of salt or sugar, or the product has been refined so far from its original state that many of the nutritional benefits have been removed.

Another great thing about the WFPB diet is how inexpensive and easy it is to shop for ingredients, especially compared to many other diets. For instance, fruits and vegetables are one of the most common whole foods you will use in this book's recipes. When shopping for frozen or canned produce, it is important to check the ingredient list for added salt and preservatives; low salt and no preservatives are preferred. Beans, legumes, and whole grains (spelt, brown rice, oats, millet, etc.) are other examples of whole ingredients. An unrefined or whole grain contains the endosperm, germ, and bran, and it provides the most nutrients and fiber. Fiber is a crucial component of a healthy and balanced diet. Even the USDA MyPlate guidelines (which are not exactly WFPB friendly) indicate that grains should make up at least a quarter of your diet. Some of my favorite grains are oats, farro, freekeh, and brown rice.

But what about white rice? Unfortunately, it has been refined, with the bran and germ removed. Brown rice is more nutrient dense and has more fiber. If you're not used to the taste of brown rice, try mixing white and brown rice together (after cooking) so you can get accustomed to the taste and texture. Another great WFPB option is black rice, which is unrefined and has a similar texture to brown rice. It also has an extremely high antioxidant count.

All this talk about grains may have you worrying about carbohydrate overload on a WFPB diet. As someone who has been on their fair share of diets, I had been conditioned to believe "carbohydrates are bad." But whole-food carbohydrates are good for us! You will see many recipes in this book using whole grains, potatoes, and starchy vegetables. I encourage you to research the difference between natural, unrefined carbohydrates and "junk food" carbs that have been refined and are laden with sugar. Unrefined carbohydrates provide the necessary fiber and energy to keep our bodies running smoothly.

When you do want to incorporate processed ingredients into your recipes, make sure the processing is minimal, with no added salt, fats, or sugars. Examples of minimally processed foods include whole-grain pasta, tofu, and unsweetened plant-based milks like soy, nut, oat, and rice milk.

Keep It (Mostly) SOS-Free

Many people who follow a WFPB diet eat "SOS-free," which means their meals contain no added salt, oil, or refined sugars. Eating meals that are SOS-free gives you the most significant health benefits, and the recipes in the book strive to stick to this approach without sacrificing flavor. However, each of the letters in "SOS" comes with its own considerations, and ultimately any decision you make about those ingredients is up to you. Even if you aren't able to stick completely to an SOS-free diet, you'll still be reaping many benefits of eating plant-based whole foods. As the saying goes, don't let perfect be the enemy of good.

S Is for Salt

It's no secret that a salt-free or low-salt diet offers many health benefits, including reduced risk of high blood pressure, heart disease, kidney damage, and diabetes. However, the bulk of processed food consumed on the standard American diet contains large amounts of salt. Additionally, many restaurant meals, especially at fast-food spots, are overloaded with salt. When cooking at home, you have the opportunity to control exactly how much salt you eat. It is this book's position that it's okay to add a little sea salt to your meals at the table, because by following a diet focused on plant-based whole foods, you're already making healthy choices. Additionally, the availability of "low-sodium" and "salt-free" canned ingredients means that you can eat as close to SOS-free as possible. While you will find ingredients like soy sauce, canned beans and tomatoes, vegetable broth, miso, and Dijon mustard in this book's recipes, you should always opt for low-sodium versions when possible. If you can't find them in your local store, check online. Just keep in mind that a can of tomatoes with a little salt added is far healthier than a pasta sauce laden with animal-derived products, sugar, and oil.

So with minimal or no salt, how will this book's recipes add flavor? Herbs and spices brighten recipes and tie ingredients together. In chapter 8 (page 123), I've included some salt-free homemade spice blends that you can make ahead of time and sprinkle on your dishes. Citrus juices and vinegar provide acidity and balance. Low-sodium soy sauce (or tamari) and miso (a fermented soybean and rice paste) add a deep umami flavor. Finally, nutritional yeast, a popular WFPB staple typically found in the spice or bulk section of the grocery store, adds a cheesy, buttery taste to dishes.

O Is for Oil

If there's one piece of information I want you to take away from this book, it's this: avoid oil. Oil is a waste of calories; it provides no nutritional benefits, and it hardens the endothelial cells of your arteries. There's currently a lot of hype around coconut oil, avocado oil, and extra-virgin olive oil. However, by eating WFPB, you'll get more nutritional value from eating a sprinkle of coconut, a quarter of an avocado, or a garnish of olives. By eating whole foods, you'll enjoy a food's actual nutrients, rather than a stripped-of-nutrients version that is high in fat.

How to Cook Without Oil

Yes, it is a learning curve to cook without oil, but once you learn and get the hang of it, you won't miss it. First step: get yourself an excellent nonstick skillet or cast-iron pan (you can still season it with oil since very little will transfer to your food while cooking).

I learned to sauté without oil by practicing with onions. Just heat your nonstick skillet or sauté pan over medium-high, and let them sizzle. At first, they'll release their own water and juices, which will keep them from sticking. Then when they start to darken, add a splash of water or vegetable stock and "deglaze" the pan, scraping up the browned bits off the bottom. If you are sweating the onions (meaning they don't need to be browned), add a little water or vegetable broth before they stick; the onions will essentially steam in the small bit of liquid. This method can be used for just about any vegetable. Plant foods with high water content, like mushrooms, will release more liquid on their own so you may not need to add any. Just keep an eye on the pan, and as you get used to the timing, you will know when to add the splash of water or broth to prevent burning or sticking.

S Is for (Refined) Sugars

Refined sugar refers to sugars that have been extracted or processed. This includes things like table and baking sugar and high-fructose corn syrup, which provide no health benefits and can lead to obesity, moodiness, and diseases like diabetes and cardiovascular disease. Focus your diet around naturally sweet and flavorful ingredients, and you won't miss the sugars. Some replacements you will find in this cookbook are dates, raisins, blackstrap molasses, and maple syrup. Additionally, you'll be relying on enhancing spices like cinnamon and ginger or add-ins like mini vegan chocolate chips or dark chocolate. Just be sure to look for dark chocolate made with whole ingredients and no added sugar and oils.

NUTRITIONAL KNOW-HOW

When I first transitioned to a WFPB diet, I often found myself in conversations about macro ingredients—protein, carbohydrates, and fats. It seemed as though everyone asked, "Where do you get your protein?" So, I did what any 21st-century gal would do. I hopped on Google and started looking into protein in a plant-based diet. My research uncovered that what I thought (and what most people think) about protein is a myth. As humans going about a typical day (not endurance athletes or bodybuilders), we need less protein than most people think, so a balanced WFPB diet provides adequate protein.

Following a combination of information from leading nutritionists and USDA guidelines, I try to stick to an 80-10-10 mix of macros—meaning 80 percent of my calories come from carbohydrates, 10 percent from protein, and 10 percent from fat. This mix has kept me full and satiated and led to significant, yet healthy, weight loss. I eat fruits, vegetables, whole grains, beans, and some nuts, seeds, and avocados within this mix. I strive to eat greens and starch at every meal, which is why I'll often have a Mango Green Smoothie (page 19) or Simple Tofu Scramble (page 26) with added spinach for breakfast.

I have found that with a balanced and varied plant-based diet, I do not need to take most supplements to meet my nutritional needs. Instead, I focus on getting the nutrients from a plant-based source, e.g., omega-3s and omega-6s from ground flaxseed and chia seeds. Many people worry about getting enough iron on a WFPB diet. But this essential mineral is plentiful in plant-based foods, including lentils, beans, hemp seeds, and quinoa. As for calcium, I tracked my intake and found it easy to achieve the recommended daily amount by eating a WFPB diet rich with green leafy vegetables, broccoli, and broccoli sprouts. The only supplement I take once a week is 2,500 milligrams of dissolvable vitamin B_{12}, which is found in animal products or added to fortified processed foods (neither of which you'll be eating on a WFPB diet). Last, it is worth mentioning that getting outside daily to soak in the vitamin D from the sun is essential to your overall health.

EAT, LIMIT, AVOID

Here are a few examples of the "always" foods that make up the base of the WFPB diet, the "sometimes" foods that are best enjoyed in moderation, and the "never" foods that shouldn't be part of the diet at all.

ALWAYS	SOMETIMES	NEVER
Whole foods eaten as close to their natural state as possible	Plant-based foods higher in fat and minimally processed plant-based foods	Animal products, processed foods, oil, refined sugar, salt*
Whole grains: rice, oats, barley, quinoa, corn **Fruits:** apples, bananas, citrus, berries, melons, stone fruit **Vegetables:** leafy greens (e.g., kale, lettuce, spinach, arugula, chard), broccoli, cauliflower, tomatoes, peppers, celery, green beans **Starchy vegetables:** potatoes, sweet potatoes, carrots, beets **Legumes:** beans, peas, lentils **Mushrooms:** portabella, shiitake, oyster, chanterelle, porcini **Aromatics:** herbs and spices, onion, garlic, ginger, turmeric	**Good fats:** nuts, seeds, avocados **Lightly processed foods:** whole-grain bread, whole-grain pasta, tofu, tempeh, soy curls **Unsweetened plant-based milks:** soy milk, almond milk, cashew milk, oat milk, rice milk **Sweeteners:** maple syrup, date paste, blackstrap molasses	**Meat:** beef, pork, chicken, lamb, venison, buffalo **Seafood:** fish, shellfish, mollusks **Dairy:** milk, butter, ghee, cheese, ice cream, whey **Eggs** **All oils:** olive oil, sesame oil, canola oil, palm oil, peanut oil, coconut oil **Processed vegan foods:** processed meat alternatives, packaged snacks, vegan ice cream

* Personally, I'm okay with occasional use of a little sea salt for finishing a dish, but many WFPB diets prohibit it.

WFPB IN JUST 30 MINUTES

You might be wondering how tasty, nutritionally sound WFPB recipes can be made in less than 30 minutes. Will you have to do all sorts of complicated cooking to get the flavors and textures you desire? Actually, the opposite is true, because you're letting the natural robust flavors of these ingredients shine in their whole forms. Plant-based foods generally take less time to cook than animal-based ones, and you won't have to worry about constantly looking at a thermometer to make sure your food is safe to eat. Even your dishes will be much quicker to wash than the oily ones from before. It's a win-win. Read on for more tips on how to make WFPB cooking fast and easy.

The Well-Stocked WFPB Kitchen

Having a kitchen stocked with WFPB staples is vital for two reasons: first, you will have ingredients on hand to create delicious and tasty meals in 30 minutes, and second, it will help keep you from eating things from the "never" section of the Always, Sometimes, Never table. Out of sight, out of mind. I try to keep my kitchen stocked with the following foods at all times. Note that some of the recipes mentioned in this section can be found in chapter 8 (page 123), which is the only section of the book in which you will encounter some recipes that take longer than 30 minutes.

Refrigerator and Freezer

Tahini is a paste or butter made from sesame seeds. It can provide a creamy base in a recipe or help thicken a sauce. It's also a great thing to drizzle on a salad dressed with vinegar.

Miso is a fermented soybean and rice paste. It comes in several varieties, including low-sodium versions. I tend to keep red miso on hand, but you may prefer white miso, which has a milder taste. If you are seeking a soy-free option, look for chickpea miso.

Tofu is bean curd that's been minimally processed (the soybeans are coagulated and pressed). You can buy it silken or extra-firm for different textures and liquid content, and it's available plain or flavored.

Unsweetened plant-based milk is made from plants, with no added sugar. It can be made from nuts, such as almonds and cashews, or from grains, such as rice and oats. I prefer shelf-stable soy milk made merely with organic soybeans and water. It works well as a coffee creamer and in baking and savory recipes.

Dijon or whole-grain mustard can help emulsify a salad dressing or add a tangy flavor to finish a dish. I find a little goes a long way, but it's always good to have on hand. Opt for low-sodium versions when you can.

Pure maple syrup can be used as a sweetener in everything from salad dressings to sauces and baked goods.

Lemon juice and lime juice are great for boosting the flavors of other foods. I keep bottles of pressed organic juice on hand since they tend to keep better than fresh citrus. Be sure to check the ingredient list; it should contain only lemon or lime juice, with no added ingredients or preservatives. If a recipe calls for the zest of a lemon or lime and I don't have one on hand, I will add an extra tablespoon of juice.

Dates are great for snacking and can be used as a sweetener or binder in baked goods. Their texture can change if they sit in the refrigerator for too long, so sometimes I will need to microwave them for about 20 seconds before blending if they are too hard.

Frozen vegetables such as corn, peas, greens, and sweet potatoes are an excellent staple to keep in the freezer to create 30-minute meals. I often use frozen corn to top a quick rice-and-bean bowl or add peas to a pasta dish.

Frozen fruits like strawberries, blueberries, mangos, and bananas make for great bases for a quick smoothie or to make a Fruit-Chia Jam (page 130).

Whole-grain bread, pitas, and wraps are something I try to always have on hand since I enjoy having a piece of toast (page 21) or a Raw Vegetable Hummus Wrap (page 65) as a quick meal or snack. I buy Food For Life's Ezekiel 4:9 whole-grain products, which can be found in the frozen food section. Since I don't eat through my bread products quickly and they lack preservatives, these products are best kept frozen.

Pantry

Nutritional yeast is deactivated yeast. It is a staple in vegan cooking due to its buttery and cheesy flavor. It's typically sold in the health food or spice section of the grocery store. You can buy it fortified with vitamin B_{12} if you prefer.

Chickpea flour (garbanzo bean flour or gram flour) is made from ground chickpeas. It is often used as a thickener in sauces.

Canned or dried beans (see Homemade Beans on page 133) can create a quick meal in a short amount of time. I've been known to heat brown rice, open a can of black beans, add salsa and a quarter of an avocado, and call it dinner. Just make sure to use low-sodium canned beans.

Vegetable broth is a staple for sautéing vegetables or flavoring grain dishes. I keep a jar of vegetable bouillon in the refrigerator or a carton of no- or low-sodium vegetable broth on hand.

Soy sauce or tamari can be used to add umami to a dish. Use tamari if you're avoiding gluten. Again, look for low-sodium versions.

Liquid amino acids are a savory condiment that can be used in sauces or to finish a dish. I tend to use it most on air-popped popcorn with a sprinkle of nutritional yeast.

Vinegar is essential for dressings and more. I have a beautiful collection of vinegars—distilled white, apple cider, red-wine, rice, and balsamic. They each have a distinctive flavor and can help brighten a dish by adding just a touch of acidity. I use vinegar (mostly balsamic and rice vinegar) plus a drizzle of tahini to dress my salad greens.

Rice, grains, oats, and other whole grains make for a great, hearty base for many quick WFPB meals. My go-to grains are oats, brown rice, and farro.

Potatoes are filling and full of vitamins. Russets and yellow potatoes are readily available in my pantry. I like to be able to throw together a quick break-fast of Simple Tofu Scramble (page 26) and Breakfast Potatoes (page 27) on any given morning.

Coconut milk is pretty much a meal in itself. Combine it with just a few other ingredients for a quick, fragrant curry or a silky soup.

Hot sauce brings the heat for those that crave it. Although I'm not a fan of spicy foods, I do keep some Frank's RedHot on hand for an impromptu Buffalo-sauce dish (or to top my popcorn). My husband, John, loves hot sauce and has quite the collection. I would caution you to read the ingredients since some brands may contain sugar and salt.

Hidden SOS Culprits

There are some sneaky foods that appear to be WFPB compliant but actually are not. Many "whole-grain" or "whole wheat" breads, for example, are not WFPB compliant because their flours go through extensive refinement. Look for breads made with sprouted grains rather than grain flour. Condiments like ketchup, barbecue sauce, dressings, and marinades can also have salt, oil, and sugars hiding in them. When reading the ingredient list, look for anything ending in *-ose* (e.g., sucrose or fructose) or anything made with corn syrup. Try to find condiments made with ingredients that are as close to whole foods as possible. Finally, another hidden culprit is lecithin, a plant-based oil often found in plant-based milk and dairy alternatives. I recommend WestSoy (soy milk) and Elmhurst (nut and grain milks), which contain no lecithin, gums, or thickeners.

6 TIME-SAVING TIPS

Use a Meal Plan

The concept is pretty self-explanatory. Write down the meals you want each night of the week ahead of time. By planning your meals, you'll cut down on time and money spent since you'll only buy what you need at the grocery store. Additionally, you can see in the following sample meal plan that I piggybacked meals with common ingredients. For example, the Cobb Salad with Tangy Red-Wine Vinaigrette (page 56) and Pasta Carbonara (page 92) both use Smoky Mushrooms (page 132), so I can double that batch and save time cooking later in the week. You can sketch out repeat ingredients and plan for lunches (especially if you eat your lunch away from home) without worrying about a time-consuming lunch prep in the morning before work. To download my weekly menu plan template, visit VegInspired.com/menuplan.

Sample Weekly Menu Plan

	BREAKFAST	LUNCH	DINNER	SNACK OR DESSERT
Sunday	Chickpea Country Gravy (page 28) with sautéed spinach	Farro Salad with Italian Vinaigrette (page 54) over mixed greens	Lentil Bolognese (page 87) with side salad	Date Balls (page 42)
Monday	Strawberry-Banana Smoothie (page 18)	Farro Salad with Italian Vinaigrette leftovers over mixed greens	Baja-Style Tacos (page 64)	White Bean Caponata (page 35) with WFPB Dippers (page 32)
Tuesday	Mango Green Smoothie (page 19)	Potato Queso Bowl (page 96)	Cobb Salad with Tangy Red-Wine Vinaigrette (page 56)	Nice Cream (page 116)
Wednesday	Chocolate Chip Cookie Oatmeal (page 24)	Raw Vegetable Hummus Wraps (page 65)	Pasta Carbonara (page 92) with side salad	Sweet Potato and Chocolate Pudding (page 104)
Thursday	Avocado Toast (page 20)	Pasta Carbonara leftovers with side salad	Vegetable Ranch Pita Pizzas (page 46)	Nice Cream (page 116)
Friday	Strawberry-Banana Smoothie (page 18)	Raw Vegetable Hummus Wraps (page 65)	Weeknight Tomato Soup (page 74) and Spinach Salad with Sweet Smoky Dressing (page 60)	Caramel-Coconut Frosted Brownies (page 110)
Saturday	Simple Tofu Scramble (page 26) and Breakfast Potatoes (page 27)	Leftover Weeknight Tomato Soup	White Jackfruit Chili (page 76)	Skillet Spinach and Artichoke Dip (page 48) and crackers

Batch-Cook Your Ingredients

By utilizing a meal plan, you can look ahead and see what ingredients you will need throughout the week. If you have a few recipes that call for cooked quinoa, you can make a double or triple batch one day and then use the cooked quinoa for future recipes that week. By batching your ingredient preparation, you save time and set yourself up for a win later in the week.

Use Precut and Precooked or Quick-Cooking Ingredients

Canned beans speed up your meals. Precut onions, celery, and peppers, which are often found in the produce section, can help you get a meal on the table in less than 30 minutes with tons of flavor. Jarred minced garlic will keep better than a head of garlic. Instant or quick-cooking grains reduce cooking time. These whole-food convenience ingredients allow you to put together a meal much faster than if you had to prep all the ingredients yourself.

Wash Your Herbs and Greens When You Get Home from the Store

I wash my herbs, cut the stem ends, and store them in a glass jar with the stems submerged in water and a reusable mesh produce bag over the top. The bag allows the herb to breathe, and it stays fresh for weeks. When washing heads of lettuce or other bulk greens, I have found using a salad spinner to spin out excess water and then storing them inside the salad spinner helps them keep their freshness in the refrigerator.

Grind Your Oats into Oat Flour in Batches

Rolled oats can be ground into oat flour in a food processor or blender. Doing this in advance allows you to grab and go for a recipe rather than break out the kitchen gadget each time. Store them properly in an airtight container.

Freeze Ingredients like Tomato Paste

Otherwise, you'll waste any excess that isn't called for in a recipe. I buy tomato paste in small cans, but some recipes don't call for the whole can. Simply take a small tablespoon scoop and freeze one-tablespoon portions of the tomato paste for future recipes.

Sweet Potato and Apple Breakfast Bowl with Maple-Tahini Sauce, page 25

CHAPTER 2

BREAKFASTS AND SMOOTHIES

STRAWBERRY-BANANA SMOOTHIE

SERVES 2
PREP TIME: 5 MINUTES

A thick and creamy smoothie is one of my favorite ways to start the day. The fruit couldn't be easier to prep, especially when you're using frozen strawberries. The addition of oats thickens the smoothie and adds a little nutrient density to help you stay satiated, while a pinch of cinnamon brightens the flavor.

1 cup unsweetened plant-based milk

1½ cups frozen strawberries

2 ripe bananas, peeled

¼ cup rolled oats

2 pitted dates

1 tablespoon ground flaxseed

⅛ teaspoon ground cinnamon

In a high-efficiency blender, combine the milk, strawberries, bananas, oats, dates, flaxseed, and cinnamon. Blend for about 30 seconds, or until smooth.

Ingredient Tip: If you don't have a high-efficiency blender, put your frozen berries in the refrigerator the night before, and microwave your dates for 20 seconds to soften them. If you prefer a thinner smoothie, increase the plant-based milk to 1½ cups.

PER SERVING: Calories: 343; Fat: 3.9g; Dietary fiber: 14.6g; Protein: 4g; Carbohydrates: 78g

MANGO GREEN SMOOTHIE

SERVES 2

PREP TIME: 5 MINUTES

Tropical notes and a hint of spinach bring this smoothie together. Using frozen mango ensures a nice creamy smoothie. Light-colored fruits, like bananas and mango, help achieve a beautiful green color. Don't like bananas? Swap out the bananas for additional mango; because it's frozen, the texture will still be creamy. Want to boost the tropical vibes? Replace a half cup of frozen mango with a half cup of frozen pineapple.

1 cup unsweetened plant-based milk

2 cups frozen mango

2 ripe bananas, peeled

1 cup packed baby spinach

3 pitted dates

½ teaspoon vanilla extract

In a high-efficiency blender, combine the milk, mango, bananas, spinach, dates, and vanilla. Blend for about 30 seconds, or until smooth.

Ingredient Tip: If you don't have a high-efficiency blender, put your frozen mango in the refrigerator the night before, and microwave your dates for 20 seconds to soften them.

PER SERVING: Calories: 282; Fat: 2.8g; Dietary fiber: 9.4g; Protein: 6.5g; Carbohydrates: 63.5g

TOAST 3 WAYS

SERVES 2

PREP TIME: 10 MINUTES

Once a breakfast afterthought, toast is now a trendy restaurant item when topped with avocado and more. Sprouted whole-grain bread (I recommend Food For Life's Ezekiel 4:9 bread) retains much of its ingredients' nutrients after manufacturing, making it a perfect complement to a WFPB diet. Here are three of my favorite ways to top it. Have more time? Try these toasts with your very own homemade Quick Spelt Bread (page 136).

AVOCADO TOAST

1 ripe avocado, pitted and quartered

4 whole-grain bread slices, toasted

1 teaspoon lemon juice

Onion powder, for seasoning

Garlic powder, for seasoning

Chia seeds, ground flaxseed, or hemp hearts, for seasoning (optional)

1. Spread a quarter of the avocado on each piece of toast.

2. Drizzle on the lemon juice.

3. Sprinkle with onion powder, garlic powder, and chia seeds (if using).

PER SERVING: Calories: 314; Fat: 14.4g; Dietary fiber: 12.1g; Protein: 10.1g; Carbohydrates: 39.5g

SAVORY SALSA TOAST

1 cup oil-free refried beans

4 whole-grain bread slices, toasted

Salsa or Pico de Gallo (page 38), for topping

Ripe avocado or Guacamole (page 39), for topping

Broccoli sprouts, for topping

Diced fresh tomatoes, for topping (optional)

1. Evenly spread about ¼ cup of refried beans on each piece of toast.

2. Add the salsa, avocado, sprouts, and tomatoes (if using).

PER SERVING: Calories: 372; Fat: 14.5g; Dietary fiber: 16.4g; Protein: 13.9g; Carbohydrates: 50.2g

"RICOTTA" & JAM TOAST

½ cup Tofu "Ricotta" (page 129)
1 to 2 tablespoons lemon juice
4 whole-grain bread slices, toasted
½ cup Fruit-Chia Jam (page 130)

1. In a small bowl, mix together the tofu ricotta and lemon juice to form a creamy paste.

2. Evenly spread the ricotta mixture on the toast.

3. Add a layer of 1 to 2 tablespoons of jam to each piece of toast.

Pair It With: Eat any of these toasts with a Mango Green Smoothie (page 19) to get your serving of greens at breakfast.

PER SERVING: Calories: 402; Fat: 11.8g; Dietary fiber: 13.7g; Protein: 21.8g; Carbohydrates: 56.8g

APPLE-CINNAMON FRENCH TOAST BAKE

SERVES 4

PREP TIME: 10 MINUTES | COOK TIME: 20 MINUTES

I love a big plate of French toast but hate cleaning up a messy griddle, so I came up with this delicious and easy recipe. By cutting the bread into chunks, letting it absorb the liquid, then baking, you get a crispy and toasty exterior with that familiar creamy interior, just like French toast off the griddle—without the mess. Serve it with fresh strawberries and bananas or a simple drizzle of pure maple syrup.

⅓ cup unsweetened applesauce

⅓ cup unsweetened soy milk

2 tablespoons pure maple syrup, plus more for serving

8 whole-grain bread slices, each cut into 9 squares

½ teaspoon ground cinnamon

¼ cup unsweetened raisins

2 tablespoons rolled oats

1. Preheat the oven to 350°F.

2. In a small bowl, mix together the applesauce, soy milk, and maple syrup.

3. Put the bread in a large bowl, and sprinkle with the cinnamon.

4. Add the raisins to the large bowl.

5. Fold in the applesauce mixture, and mix well until the bread absorbs the liquid.

6. Transfer the bread mixture evenly into an 8-by-8-inch glass baking dish.

7. Sprinkle the top with the oats.

8. Bake for about 20 minutes, or until the top is golden brown and crispy. Remove from the oven.

9. Divide the French toast among 4 plates. Serve each with 1 to 2 tablespoons of maple syrup.

Variation Tip: Want to jazz this up? Use whole-grain cinnamon-raisin bread, or mix ¼ cup of unsalted nuts into the bread mixture in step 4.

PER SERVING: Calories: 352; Fat: 1.7g; Dietary fiber: 6.9g; Protein: 9.1g; Carbohydrates: 77.1g

CHOCOLATE CHIP COOKIE OATMEAL

SERVES 2

PREP TIME: 5 MINUTES | COOK TIME: 10 MINUTES

On a chilly morning, there's nothing better than breakfasting on a bowl of warm oats. Simmering the oats with vanilla and maple syrup yields a comforting cookie-flavored oatmeal. I add vegan chocolate chips to my oats, but shaved dark chocolate or cocoa nibs would be a tasty alternative. Oatmeal for breakfast keeps me satiated for hours and is a great way to start the day with a hearty, heart-friendly helping of fiber. This recipe tastes more like a dessert cup than breakfast and also makes for a great snack.

2 cups unsweetened soy milk

2 tablespoons pure maple syrup

1 teaspoon vanilla extract

1 cup rolled oats

1 tablespoon ground flaxseed or flax meal

2 tablespoons mini vegan chocolate chips or shaved dark chocolate

1. In a small saucepan, combine the soy milk, maple syrup, and vanilla. Bring to a boil.

2. Reduce the heat to medium. Add the oats, and simmer for 5 to 7 minutes, or until the oatmeal has thickened. Remove from the heat.

3. Stir in the flaxseed, and let sit for 1 to 2 minutes.

4. Divide the oatmeal and chocolate chips between bowls.

Variation Tip: The oatmeal base welcomes any creative cookie toppings you want. Try it with raisins in place of the chocolate chips. Reduce the amount of chocolate, and add coconut, nuts, and raisins. Or replace the chocolate chips with Fruit-Chia Jam (page 130) or fresh fruit for a thumbprint cookie style of oatmeal.

PER SERVING: Calories: 444; Fat: 13.1g; Dietary fiber: 7.6g; Protein: 15g; Carbohydrates: 66.8g

SWEET POTATO AND APPLE BREAKFAST BOWL WITH MAPLE-TAHINI SAUCE

SERVES 2

PREP TIME: 5 MINUTES | COOK TIME: 15 MINUTES

Sweet potato and apple simmered in vanilla-infused water is a simple delight to the senses. The maple-tahini sauce adds a depth of flavor while keeping the overall dish light and sweet. Having sweet potatoes for breakfast starts your day with a big serving of healthy vegetables and should keep you full until lunch.

2 tablespoons pure maple syrup

2 tablespoons tahini

½ cup water

½ teaspoon vanilla extract

1½ cups quartered sliced (½-inch) sweet potato

1½ cups diced (½-inch) Granny Smith apple

2 tablespoons unsweetened raisins

2 tablespoons walnut pieces

⅛ teaspoon ground cinnamon

1. In a small bowl, whisk together the maple syrup and tahini into a sauce.

2. In a sauté pan or skillet, stir together the water and vanilla.

3. Add the sweet potato and apple. Cover and simmer over medium-low heat for 12 to 15 minutes, or until a knife slides easily into the sweet potato. Remove from the heat.

4. Stir in the raisins, walnuts, and cinnamon.

5. Serve the bowls drizzled with the maple-tahini sauce.

Ingredient Tip: Using crisp and firm Granny Smith apples yields a nice texture. Softer apple varieties will become mushy if cooked for the whole time, so they should be added halfway through the cooking process.

PER SERVING: Calories: 443; Fat: 13.3g; Dietary fiber: 11.4g; Protein: 8.2g; Carbohydrates: 78.9g

SIMPLE TOFU SCRAMBLE

SERVES 2 TO 4

PREP TIME: 5 MINUTES | COOK TIME: 15 MINUTES

Tofu scramble has been one of my go-to breakfasts since adopting a plant-based way of eating. Tofu can be a little bland on its own, but scramble it with spices and herbs, and you've got yourself a flavorful breakfast. To vary the recipe, you can add a few cups of fresh spinach toward the end of the cooking time, letting it wilt and cook into the scramble.

2 tablespoons red miso paste

½ cup water

2 (14-ounce) packages firm tofu, drained

2 tablespoons onion powder

2 tablespoons nutritional yeast

1 teaspoon dried parsley

½ teaspoon garlic powder

¼ teaspoon ground turmeric

¼ teaspoon freshly ground black pepper

1. In a sauté pan or skillet, dissolve the miso in the water.

2. Loosely crumble the tofu into the miso-water mixture.

3. Stir in the onion powder, nutritional yeast, parsley, garlic powder, turmeric, and pepper. Cook over medium heat, stirring occasionally, for 10 to 15 minutes, or until heated through and most of the liquid has been absorbed. Remove from the heat.

Pair It With: Serve this with Breakfast Potatoes (page 27) or a slice of Quick Spelt Bread (page 136). You can also use it as the filling for a breakfast burrito or taco accompanied by black beans and Pico de Gallo & Guacamole (page 38).

PER SERVING: Calories: 84; Fat: 2.4g; Dietary fiber: 2.3g; Protein: 7.2g; Carbohydrates: 8.8g

BREAKFAST POTATOES

SERVES 4 TO 6

PREP TIME: 10 MINUTES | COOK TIME: 20 MINUTES

Missing traditional home fries for breakfast? For this WFPB-approved version, I omit the oil, amp up the flavor using vegetable broth and herbs and spices, and cook the potatoes to perfection. These potatoes are a great staple to batch-cook and eat as leftovers, especially when you need to use up a bag of potatoes sitting in the pantry.

1½ pounds Yukon gold potatoes, cut into ½-inch-thick slices, then cut into bite-size pieces

½ cup vegetable broth

1 teaspoon dried parsley

¼ teaspoon freshly ground black pepper

½ teaspoon garlic powder

½ teaspoon onion powder

½ teaspoon paprika

¼ teaspoon dried sage

¼ teaspoon dried thyme

1. In a nonstick sauté pan or skillet, combine the potatoes, broth, parsley, and pepper. Bring to a simmer over medium heat. Cover and cook for about 15 to 20 minutes, or until a knife slides easily into the potatoes. Remove from the heat.

2. While the potatoes cook, in a small bowl, mix together the garlic powder, onion powder, paprika, sage, and thyme.

3. Off the heat, sprinkle the spice mixture over the potatoes, and stir to coat evenly.

Pair It With: Serve this as a big plate of potatoes with my homemade Ketchup (page 127) or alongside a Simple Tofu Scramble (page 26).

PER SERVING: Calories: 95; Fat: 0.2g; Dietary fiber: 1.9g; Protein: 3.1g; Carbohydrates: 21.4g

CHICKPEA COUNTRY GRAVY

SERVES 4 TO 6

PREP TIME: 10 MINUTES | COOK TIME: 10 MINUTES

This recipe is inspired by my time living in Charlotte, North Carolina, and the Southern breakfasts I used to enjoy there. Creamy and seasoned with sage and fennel, it has all the flavors of a sausage gravy, without the sausage. This gravy can be served over Breakfast Potatoes (page 27), an oil-free biscuit, or a whole-grain English muffin.

8 ounces silken tofu

½ cup unsweetened soy milk

2 tablespoons chickpea flour

1 (15-ounce) can chickpeas, drained and rinsed

1 tablespoon dried sage

2 teaspoons liquid aminos

1 teaspoon freshly ground black pepper

½ teaspoon ground fennel

1. In a blender, combine the tofu, soy milk, and chickpea flour. Blend until smooth.

2. In a sauté pan or skillet, combine the tofu mixture, chickpeas, sage, liquid aminos, pepper, and fennel. Bring to a simmer. Cook for about 5 minutes, or until thickened. Remove from the heat.

Variation Tip: A sliced fresh summer tomato or a cup of fruit adds brightness to a meal with gravy.

PER SERVING: Calories: 115; Fat: 2.8g; Dietary fiber: 3.1g; Protein: 8.3g; Carbohydrates: 14.2g

CREAMY CORN GRITS
WITH KALE AND MUSHROOMS

SERVES 4 TO 6

PREP TIME: 5 MINUTES | COOK TIME: 20 MINUTES

Creamy grits (or polenta) paired with savory mushrooms provide a nice balanced breakfast. Grits are typically laden with butter and cream to yield an extra creamy and rich flavor. You can achieve a similar effect using unsweetened plant-based milk and nutritional yeast. I like to use yellow corn grits (also called polenta), but white grits can be used as well. This recipe works well with fresh or frozen kale or spinach. Serve this dish with your favorite hot sauce.

8 ounces cremini mushrooms, cut into ½-inch-thick slices

1 tablespoon water, plus 2 cups, divided

2 cups unsweetened plant-based milk

½ cup dry-packed, oil-free sun-dried tomatoes, sliced

2 tablespoons nutritional yeast

2 teaspoons onion powder

¼ teaspoon garlic powder

1 cup corn grits

3 cups chopped green kale

1 cup Tofu "Ricotta" (page 129)

¼ teaspoon freshly ground black pepper

1. In a sauté pan or skillet, combine the mushrooms and 1 tablespoon of water. Sauté over medium-high heat for about 5 minutes, or until the mushrooms have browned.

2. Add the plant-based milk, remaining 2 cups of water, the tomatoes, nutritional yeast, onion powder, and garlic powder.

3. Increase the heat to high. Bring to a boil. Stir in the grits and kale.

4. Reduce the heat to low. Cook, stirring occasionally, for 5 to 7 minutes, or until the grits are creamy. Remove from the heat.

5. Stir in the ricotta and pepper.

PER SERVING: Calories: 483; Fat: 19.9g; Dietary fiber: 11.2g; Protein: 46.7g; Carbohydrates: 32g

Oatmeal Granola Bar Bites, page 44

CHAPTER 3

SNACKS

WFPB DIPPERS

SERVES 2 TO 4

PREP TIME: 5 MINUTES | COOK TIME: 25 MINUTES

These are for my fellow snacking fans (and, I mean, who isn't one?). When dining out, I am drawn to crostini, chips, or anything else I can dip. Sadly, most of the typical handheld snack scoopers out there are highly processed or include not-so-great ingredients. Enter my WFPB-approved dippers. These make for the perfect vessel for Skillet Spinach and Artichoke Dip (page 48), White Bean Dip 3 Ways (page 34), Pico de Gallo & Guacamole (page 38), or your favorite dip.

TOAST POINTS

8 whole-grain bread slices (thawed if frozen)

Balsamic vinegar, for brushing (optional)

Garlic powder, for seasoning

1. Lay the bread flat on a parchment-lined baking sheet.

2. Brush the bread with a thin layer of vinegar (if using).

3. Sprinkle with garlic powder.

4. Transfer the baking sheet to a cold oven, and heat to 350°F.

5. When the oven reaches temperature, flip the bread over. Bake for another 5 to 15 minutes, or until crispy to your liking. Remove from the oven.

PER SERVING: Calories: 165; Fat: 1g; Dietary fiber: 6.1g; Protein: 8.2g; Carbohydrates: 31.1g

TORTILLA CHIPS

4 to 6 oil-free corn tortillas, cut
    into triangles

1. Spread the tortilla triangles
   out in a single layer on a
   parchment-lined baking sheet.

2. Transfer the baking sheet to a
   cold oven, and heat to 350°F.

3. When the oven reaches temperature, flip the tortillas over. Bake
   for another 10 to 15 minutes, or
   until crispy.

Variation Tip: I toast my corn tortillas plain, but you can brush them lightly with
lime juice and sprinkle on a little Chili Spice Blend (page 124).

PER SERVING: Calories: 180; Fat: 3g; Dietary fiber: 4.5g; Protein: 4.5g; Carbohydrates: 34.5g

PITA CHIPS

4 to 6 whole-grain pita breads, cut
    into triangles

1. Spread the pita triangles
   out in a single layer on a
   parchment-lined baking sheet.

2. Transfer the baking sheet to a
   cold oven, and heat to 350°F.

3. When the oven reaches temperature, flip the pitas over. Bake
   for another 10 to 15 minutes, or
   until crispy.

PER SERVING: Calories: 150; Fat: 0.8g; Dietary fiber: 6g; Protein: 10.5g; Carbohydrates: 31.5g

WHITE BEAN DIP 3 WAYS

SERVES 4 TO 6

PREP TIME: 10 MINUTES

Mild-mannered white beans are the star of these three recipes. With their creamy texture and pleasant flavor, they mix well with a variety of ingredients. I love to make these dips and store them in the refrigerator to grab as a quick snack. They pair well with any of the WFPB Dippers (page 32).

WHITE BEAN BRUSCHETTA

1 (15-ounce) can reduced-sodium white beans, drained and rinsed

2 cups diced tomatoes

½ cup packed fresh basil, chiffonade

3 tablespoons balsamic vinegar

½ teaspoon garlic powder

In a medium bowl, combine the beans, tomatoes, basil, vinegar, and garlic powder. Using a rubber spatula or wooden spoon, mix gently.

PER SERVING: Calories: 102; Fat: 0.2g; Dietary fiber: 4.9g; Protein: 6.1g; Carbohydrates: 18.9g

LEMON-PEPPER BEAN DIP WITH ROSEMARY

1 (15-ounce) can reduced-sodium white beans, drained and rinsed

1 tablespoon lemon juice

1 tablespoon red-wine vinegar

1 teaspoon freshly ground black pepper

½ teaspoon garlic powder

½ teaspoon dried rosemary

Pinch red pepper flakes

In a medium bowl, combine the beans, lemon juice, vinegar, pepper, garlic powder, rosemary, and red pepper flakes. Gently mix until combined (although this dip can be mixed and slightly mashed to create a chunkier texture).

PER SERVING: Calories: 88; Fat: 0.1g; Dietary fiber: 4g; Protein: 5.4g; Carbohydrates: 15.7g

WHITE BEAN CAPONATA

¼ cup dry-packed, oil-free
   sun-dried tomatoes

1 (15-ounce) can reduced-sodium
   white beans, drained and rinsed

½ cup unsweetened raisins

¼ cup grated carrot

¼ cup water-packed roasted red pepper

¼ cup green olives with pimentos

3 tablespoon red-wine vinegar

2 tablespoons pine nuts, toasted

2 tablespoons capers, drained

1. In a small bowl, cover the sun-dried tomatoes with water, and let sit for 5 to 7 minutes, or until soft. Drain, and chop the tomatoes.

2. In a medium bowl, combine the sun-dried tomatoes, beans, raisins, carrot, roasted red pepper, olives, vinegar, pine nuts, and capers. Using a wooden spoon or spatula, mix gently.

Ingredient Tip: Using canned beans is definitely faster, but making these using Homemade Beans (page 133) is a delicious option.

PER SERVING: Calories: 182; Fat: 4.1g; Dietary fiber: 7g; Protein: 7.5g; Carbohydrates: 32.1g

OIL-FREE HUMMUS

MAKES 1½ CUPS

PREP TIME: 10 MINUTES

Homemade hummus paired with fresh vegetables, WFPB Dippers (page 32), or Mary's Gone Crackers brand is one of my go-to snacks. I typically make my hummus with Homemade Beans (page 133), but canned beans work for a faster option. I always have a batch of hummus on hand for my afternoon snack or a quick Raw Vegetable Hummus Wrap (page 65).

BASIC OIL-FREE HUMMUS

1 (15-ounce) can chickpeas, drained and rinsed

1 tablespoon tahini

¼ teaspoon garlic powder

¼ teaspoon ground cumin

¼ cup lemon juice

¹⁄₁₆ teaspoon cayenne

¼ teaspoon za'atar

In a food processor, combine the chickpeas, tahini, garlic powder, cumin, lemon juice, cayenne, and za'atar. Process until smooth and creamy.

PER SERVING (1 TABLESPOON): Calories: 136; Fat: 5.6g; Dietary fiber: 3.3g; Protein: 3g; Carbohydrates: 21.2g

ROMESCO-STYLE HUMMUS

1 teaspoon dry-packed, oil-free
    sun-dried tomato

1 (15-ounce) can chickpeas, drained
    and rinsed

¼ cup water-packed roasted red pepper

3 tablespoons balsamic vinegar

2 tablespoons sliced or slivered almonds

¼ teaspoon garlic powder

¼ teaspoon onion powder

⅛ teaspoon smoked paprika

1. In a bowl, reconstitute
   the sun-dried tomato in
   water. Drain.

2. In a food processor, combine the
   sun-dried tomato, chickpeas,
   roasted red pepper, vinegar,
   almonds, garlic powder, onion
   powder, and paprika. Process
   until smooth and creamy.

Variation Tip: Add ¼ teaspoon curry powder to the basic oil-free hummus to give it more pep.

PER SERVING (1 TABLESPOON): Calories: 105; Fat: 2g; Dietary fiber: 4.9g; Protein: 5.5g; Carbohydrates: 17g

PICO DE GALLO & GUACAMOLE

SERVES 4 TO 6

PREP TIME: 20 MINUTES

Fresh dips like these are perfect to pair with Tortilla Chips (see the WFPB Dippers recipe on page 32). The guacamole also goes well with sliced cucumber as a dipper. Both dips will keep for a couple of days in the refrigerator. When choosing an avocado, look for one that is soft to the touch at the stem end. I store any unripe avocados on the counter until they reach the desired softness and then I refrigerate them until I'm ready to use them.

PICO DE GALLO

1 cup finely diced tomatoes

½ cup diced peeled English cucumber or seeded cucumber

½ cup white onion, diced and rinsed

¼ cup chopped fresh cilantro

2 tablespoons minced seeded serrano pepper

Juice of 1 lime (about 2 tablespoons)

In a medium bowl, using a wooden spoon or rubber spatula, mix together the tomatoes, cucumber, onion, cilantro, serrano pepper, and lime.

PER SERVING: Calories: 20; Fat: 0.1g; Dietary fiber: 1.3g; Protein: 0.9g; Carbohydrates: 4.8g

GUACAMOLE

4 ripe avocados, pitted and
 peeled, divided
2 tablespoons chopped fresh cilantro
1 tablespoon lime juice
⅛ teaspoon garlic powder

1. In a medium bowl, using a fork, mash 3 of the avocados until creamy. Chop the remaining avocado.

2. Gently stir in the cilantro, lime juice, garlic powder, and chopped avocado.

Storage Tip: To store the guacamole, press plastic wrap directly onto the dip and then seal in an airtight container.

PER SERVING: Calories: 195; Fat: 17.8g; Dietary fiber: 7.9g; Protein: 2.3g; Carbohydrates: 10.6g

VANILLA-CINNAMON FRUIT COCKTAIL

SERVES 4 TO 6
PREP TIME: 10 MINUTES

Fresh fruit enhanced with a hint of vanilla and lemon makes this a grown-up version of your favorite fruit cocktail. Store-bought fruit cocktails often contain added sugar, so in this version I play up the sweetness of the fruits and draw out their juices with chia seeds. This mélange of fruit is perfect as a snack on its own or served alongside pancakes or waffles for breakfast.

1 pint blueberries

2 cups diced Granny Smith apples

1 cup halved mandarin orange slices

1 cup sliced strawberries

2 tablespoons lemon juice

2 tablespoons chia seeds

½ teaspoon vanilla extract

¼ teaspoon ground cinnamon

In a large bowl, using a wooden spoon or rubber spatula, mix together the blueberries, apples, orange slices, strawberries, lemon juice, chia seeds, vanilla, and cinnamon. Serve immediately, or refrigerate until serving.

Variation Tip: Mix and match your fresh fruit; add grapes, pineapple, or jicama for a unique twist.

PER SERVING: Calories: 114; Fat: 2g; Dietary fiber: 5.8g; Protein: 2g; Carbohydrates: 25.4g

SKILLET CAULIFLOWER BITES

SERVES 4 TO 6

PREP TIME: 5 MINUTES | COOK TIME: 15 MINUTES

Growing up in western New York State, Buffalo and barbecue wings were a common treat in my home. As a WFPB alternative, cooked cauliflower florets resemble the shape of a drumette and provide an excellent texture for a wing-like snack. I love them dipped in my Homemade Barbecue Sauce (page 126), store-bought hot sauce, and tofu ranch dip (see the Vegetable Ranch Pita Pizzas recipe on page 46).

1 head cauliflower, cut into 1½- to 2-inch florets

In a nonstick skillet, cook the cauliflower over medium heat, stirring every 3 to 5 minutes, for about 15 minutes, or until browned and crisp-tender. Remove from the heat.

Ingredient Tip: You can also roast the cauliflower in 400°F oven on a parchment paper–lined baking sheet for 20 minutes, flipping halfway through, or until crisp-tender.

PER SERVING: Calories: 36; Fat: 0.1g; Dietary fiber: 3.6g; Protein: 2.9g; Carbohydrates: 7.6g

DATE BALLS

MAKES 24 (1-TABLESPOON) DATE BALLS
PREP TIME: 10 MINUTES

These sweet grab-and-go snacks come together quickly. Dates help these tasty treats stick together and add a hint of caramel flavor. The savory oat-nut mixture is enlivened by the freshness of shredded carrots (in the first recipe) and sweet, juicy strawberries (in the second).

CARROT CAKE DATE BALLS

1 cup shredded carrots
1 cup pitted dates
½ cup walnut pieces
¼ cup rolled oats
1 tablespoon coconut flakes
½ teaspoon ground cinnamon
¼ teaspoon ground ginger
⅛ teaspoon ground cloves
⅛ teaspoon ground nutmeg

1. Line a plate with parchment paper.

2. In a food processor, combine the carrots, dates, walnuts, oats, coconut flakes, ginger, cloves, and nutmeg. Process until a paste forms.

3. Using a 1-tablespoon scoop, form the paste into balls.

4. Place the balls in a single layer on the prepared plate. Serve immediately, or refrigerate in an airtight container for up to 5 days.

PER SERVING: Calories: 43; Fat: 1.7g; Dietary fiber: 1g; Protein: 1g; Carbohydrates: 7g

STRAWBERRY-PISTACHIO DATE BALLS

¾ cup pitted dates

¾ cup rolled oats, divided

½ cup strawberries

1 tablespoon ground flaxseed

½ teaspoon vanilla extract

½ cup no-salt roasted pistachios

1. Line a plate with parchment paper.

2. In a food processor, combine the dates, ½ cup of oats, the strawberries, flaxseed, vanilla, and pistachios. Process until a paste forms.

3. Stir in the remaining ¼ cup of oats.

4. Using a 1-tablespoon scoop, form the paste into balls.

5. Place the balls in a single layer on the prepared plate. Serve immediately, or refrigerate in an airtight container for up to 5 days.

Ingredient Tip: If the dates are hard, microwave for 20 seconds to soften them.

PER SERVING: Calories: 36; Fat: 0.9g; Dietary fiber: 1g; Protein: 0.9g; Carbohydrates: 6.5g

OATMEAL GRANOLA BAR BITES

SERVES 12

PREP TIME: 5 MINUTES | COOK TIME: 25 MINUTES

Granola bars make for a hearty snack on the go, but store-bought bars can be loaded with oodles of non-WFPB ingredients. Making them at home allows you to control what you put in them, and they are tastier. Using parchment paper to line your baking sheet will keep these from sticking to the pan when they bake. And make sure to use natural peanut butter with no added sugar.

1½ cups rolled oats

⅓ cup unsweetened applesauce

¼ cup unsweetened natural peanut butter

2 tablespoons pure maple syrup

2 tablespoons ground flaxseed

1 tablespoon finely chopped pecans

1 tablespoon sliced almonds

1 tablespoon unsweetened raisins

1 tablespoon mini vegan chocolate chips

1. Preheat the oven to 350°F. Line an 8-by-8-inch baking dish and a baking sheet with parchment paper.

2. In a large bowl, using a wooden spoon or rubber spatula, mix together the oats, applesauce, peanut butter, maple syrup, flaxseed, pecans, almonds, raisins, and chocolate chips.

3. Using the back of a measuring cup, firmly press the mixture into the prepared baking dish.

4. Lift the pressed mixture out, and cut into 12 equal pieces.

5. Place the cut pieces in single layer on the prepared baking sheet.

6. Transfer the baking sheet to the oven, and bake for 20 to 25 minutes, flipping halfway through, or until the bars are golden brown. Remove from the oven.

Variation Tip: Change up your granola bar bites by using different nut butters, nuts, and dried fruits.

PER SERVING: Calories: 98; Fat: 4.6g; Dietary fiber: 1.9g; Protein: 3.2g; Carbohydrates: 12.4g

VEGETABLE RANCH PITA PIZZAS

SERVES 2
PREP TIME: 10 MINUTES | COOK TIME: 15 MINUTES

I used to enjoy making pizzas as a party snack using crescent roll dough from the pop-open cans and topping them with ranch dip and raw veggies. Needless to say, those days are long gone. But these WFPB-approved pita pizzas are just as good. The slightly crispy whole-grain pitas topped with a flavorful ranch dip and loaded with vegetables make for a perfect anytime snack. I keep the ranch dip and chopped vegetables on hand in the refrigerator so I can whip up a pita pizza in no time. Make sure to use pita bread that's 100 percent whole grain.

For the tofu ranch dip

1 (14-ounce) container firm tofu, drained
¼ cup apple cider vinegar
2 tablespoons nutritional yeast
2 tablespoons dried dill
2 tablespoons lemon juice
1 tablespoon red miso paste
1 tablespoon onion powder
2 teaspoons garlic powder
1 teaspoon dried parsley
½ teaspoon paprika
¼ teaspoon celery seed

For the pitas

4 whole-grain pita breads
½ cup finely chopped broccoli florets
½ cup sliced red bell pepper
½ cup grated carrot
½ cup diced tomatoes
¼ cup finely chopped pitted olives

To make the tofu ranch dip

1. In a medium bowl, mix together the tofu, vinegar, nutritional yeast, dill, lemon juice, miso, onion powder, garlic powder, parsley, paprika, and celery seed.

To make the pitas

2. Line a baking sheet with parchment paper.

3. Place the pitas on the prepared baking sheet.

4. Transfer the baking sheet to a cold oven, and heat to 350°F. Once the oven reaches temperature, bake the pitas for another 5 minutes. Remove from the oven.

5. Flip the pitas over onto plates, crispy side on the bottom.

6. Spread ¼ cup of tofu ranch dip evenly onto each pita.

7. Divide the broccoli, bell pepper, carrot, tomatoes, and olives among the 4 pitas.

PER SERVING: Calories: 268; Fat: 6.6g; Dietary fiber: 7.1g; Protein: 12.5g; Carbohydrates: 44.5g

SKILLET SPINACH AND ARTICHOKE DIP

SERVES 6

PREP TIME: 10 MINUTES | COOK TIME: 15 MINUTES

Creamy, cheesy, and packed with spinach and artichokes, this dip will be a hit at any gathering or can be enjoyed as a snack. Most dairy cheeses add a lot of salt to dishes, so to round out the flavor I add vegetable broth and a good helping of nutritional yeast and spices. Serve this with WFPB crackers (I recommend Mary's Gone Crackers brand) or rice cakes, as a toast or baked potato topping, or as the filling in a quesadilla.

8 ounces silken tofu

½ cup soy milk

2 tablespoons chickpea flour

¼ cup vegetable broth

10 ounces frozen spinach

1 (12-ounce) jar plain artichoke hearts, chopped

¼ cup nutritional yeast

2 teaspoons liquid aminos

1 teaspoon onion powder

1 teaspoon garlic powder

1. In a blender, combine the tofu, soy milk, and flour. Blend until smooth.

2. In a sauté pan, heat the broth over medium heat. Add the spinach, and bring to a simmer. Cover, and cook for 4 to 5 minutes.

3. Add the tofu mixture, artichoke hearts, nutritional yeast, liquid aminos, onion powder, and garlic powder. Simmer, stirring occasionally, for 5 to 7 minutes, or until thickened. Remove from the heat.

Variation Tip: This dip makes a great filling for stuffed mushrooms. Preheat the oven to 350°F. Lay the mushrooms (stems removed), stem-side up, on a parchment paper–lined baking sheet. Fill them with dip, and bake for 15 to 20 minutes, or until the mushrooms are cooked and the filling starts to turn golden brown on top.

PER SERVING: Calories: 143; Fat: 1.9g; Dietary fiber: 11g; Protein: 12.1g; Carbohydrates: 19.8g

Portabella Mushroom Sandwiches with Pesto "Ricotta," page 68

CHAPTER 4

SALADS AND HANDHELDS

BEET, CABBAGE, AND BLACK BEAN SALAD

SERVES 4 TO 6
PREP TIME: 5 MINUTES | COOK TIME: 20 MINUTES

Simmered beets tossed in a tangy vinegar are a perfect topping for a whole grain like brown rice or farro. The firm, yet soft texture of the warm beets contrasts with the fresh crunch of the cabbage and creates a balanced and delicious mouthfeel. Fresh avocado finishes the dish on a creamy note.

3 or 4 medium beets, peeled and cut into ½-inch dice

½ cup water

1 (15-ounce) can black beans, drained and rinsed

1 cup shredded cabbage

1 cup shredded spinach

1 cup halved grape tomatoes

2 scallions, green and white parts, thinly sliced

½ cup seasoned rice vinegar

¼ teaspoon freshly ground black pepper

4 to 6 cups cooked brown rice

1 ripe avocado, pitted, peeled, and diced

Fresh cilantro, for garnish

1. In a sauté pan or skillet, combine the beets and water. Bring to a simmer over high heat.

2. Reduce the heat to medium-low. Cover, and cook for 10 to 15 minutes, or until the beets are slightly soft. Remove from the heat.

3. Stir in the beans, cabbage, spinach, tomatoes, scallions, vinegar, and pepper.

4. Serve the vegetables over the rice.

5. Top with the avocado, and garnish with cilantro.

Ingredient Tip: I like to cook my brown rice in a rice cooker, but there are a multitude of quick-cooking brown rice brands on the market. Some are ready in less than 20 minutes.

PER SERVING: Calories: 179; Fat: 7g; Dietary fiber: 9.5g; Protein: 6.7g; Carbohydrates: 25.5g

KALE WITH CREAMY GARLIC-DIJON DRESSING

SERVES 4

PREP TIME: 15 MINUTES

There is no denying the health benefits of kale, but the tough texture can be difficult for many to get around. In this recipe, I share with you a tip to achieve perfectly tender kale and a creamy dressing that's rich enough to stand up to this hearty green.

For the kale

1 bunch curly leaf kale (about 8 cups kale leaves)

For the dressing

¾ cup water

¼ cup raw cashews

¼ cup lemon juice

2 garlic cloves

2 tablespoons chia seeds

1 pitted date

1 tablespoon Dijon mustard

1 teaspoon red miso paste

¼ teaspoon garlic powder

⅛ teaspoon ground turmeric

To make the kale

1. Wash the kale, and remove the stems.

2. In a large bowl, gently massage the kale for 8 to 10 minutes, remove any remaining hard stems, and tear the kale into bite-size pieces.

To make the dressing

3. In a high-speed blender, combine the water, cashews, lemon juice, garlic, chia seeds, date, mustard, miso, garlic powder, and turmeric. Blend for 30 seconds.

4. Pour the dressing into the bowl, and toss the kale to coat. Serve immediately.

Ingredient Tip: Massaging the kale by gently squeezing the leaves will break down the leaf structure, leaving tender greens. The process may seem tedious, but the result is delicious and easy-to-chew kale.

PER SERVING: Calories: 163; Fat: 6.6g; Dietary fiber: 5.3g; Protein: 7.5g; Carbohydrates: 22.5g

FARRO SALAD WITH ITALIAN VINAIGRETTE

SERVES 4 TO 6
PREP TIME: 10 MINUTES

This scrumptious farro salad is adapted from my favorite pasta salad with Italian dressing. Loaded with vegetables and a tangy dressing and served cold, it is a refreshing meal on a hot day. This salad is even better the second day, after the farro has started to absorb the dressing and the vegetables break down to crisp and tender bites. Prepare this dish for a summer picnic or a make-ahead lunch. I like to use an English cucumber or remove the seeds from a standard cucumber.

For the vinaigrette

- ⅔ cup aquafaba (liquid from 1 can chickpeas)
- ⅓ cup red-wine vinegar
- 2 tablespoons Italian Seasoning (page 124)
- 2 tablespoons nutritional yeast
- 1 tablespoon red miso paste
- ½ teaspoon garlic powder
- ½ teaspoon onion powder
- ½ teaspoon paprika

To make the vinaigrette

1. In a small bowl or container with a lid, combine the aquafaba, vinegar, Italian seasoning, nutritional yeast, miso, garlic powder, onion powder, and paprika. Whisk vigorously or shake.

For the salad

2 cups cooked farro, chilled

1 (15-ounce) can chickpeas, strained (reserve the liquid for the dressing) and rinsed

1 cup diced peeled cucumber

1 cup halved grape tomatoes

½ cup diced red bell pepper

½ cup chopped broccoli florets

½ cup sliced green olives with pimentos

½ cup sliced black olives

To make the salad

2. In a large bowl, combine the farro, chickpeas, cucumber, tomatoes, bell pepper, broccoli, green olives, and black olives. Using a wooden spoon or rubber spatula, gently mix together.

3. Pour the dressing over the salad, and stir to coat. If you're making for the next day, refrigerate until ready to serve.

Variation Tip: Serve a scoop of this on a bed of mixed greens for a unique salad.

PER SERVING: Calories: 497; Fat: 13.4g; Dietary fiber: 14.3g; Protein: 14.8g; Carbohydrates: 74.7g

COBB SALAD WITH TANGY RED-WINE VINAIGRETTE

SERVES 4

PREP TIME: 10 MINUTES

Chock-full of fresh vegetables, beans, and grains, this salad has all the ingredients for a balanced meal on its own. Traditional Cobb salad includes egg, bacon, and blue cheese, all WFPB no-nos. In this adaptation, I substitute those ingredients with chickpeas, Smoky Mushrooms (page 132), and a tangy red-wine vinaigrette that has a hint of that blue cheese flavor without the animal products or fatty cheese.

For the vinaigrette

⅔ cup aquafaba (liquid from 1 can chickpeas)

⅓ cup red-wine vinegar

¼ cup tahini

2 teaspoons red miso paste

1 teaspoon nutritional yeast

½ teaspoon dried dill

½ teaspoon dried parsley

½ teaspoon celery seed

½ teaspoon ground mustard

½ teaspoon garlic powder

To make the vinaigrette

1. In a small bowl or container with a lid, combine the aquafaba, vinegar, tahini, miso, nutritional yeast, dill, parsley, celery seed, mustard, and garlic powder. Whisk vigorously or shake.

For the salad

1 (5-ounce) container mixed
    baby greens

1 batch Smoky Mushrooms (page 132)

1 ripe avocado, pitted, peeled,
    and sliced

1 cup sliced cooked beets

1 cup halved grape tomatoes

1 (15-ounce) can chickpeas, strained
    (reserve the liquid for the dressing)
    and rinsed

2 cups cooked quinoa

Freshly ground black pepper

To make the salad

2. Evenly divide the greens, mush-
    rooms, avocado, beets, tomatoes,
    chickpeas, and quinoa among
    4 salad bowls or plates.

3. Drizzle ¼ cup of the vinaigrette
    per bowl. Season with pepper.

Variation Tip: Don't love quinoa? Substitute farro or freekeh for a nutty,
whole-grain option.

PER SERVING: Calories: 617; Fat: 24.1g; Dietary fiber: 14.3g; Protein: 21.8g; Carbohydrates: 82.5g

BULGUR LETTUCE CUPS

SERVES 2 TO 4

PREP TIME: 10 MINUTES | COOK TIME: 20 MINUTES

Umami-seasoned bulgur (a Middle Eastern whole grain) paired with the crisp fresh bite of lettuce and sweet tangy peanut sauce makes this one of my favorite recipes in this cookbook. I love how easy it is to mix together the filling. I use red leaf lettuce because it stays fresh longer in the refrigerator. For the cabbage, consider keeping a head of red cabbage in a reusable mesh produce bag in the crisper drawer. You can take it apart a leaf at a time whenever you want to use some. I have had some heads of cabbage stay fresh for a few weeks stored this way. Want to turn up the heat? Simply increase the amount of red pepper flakes or add more sriracha.

For the sauce

½ cup unsweetened natural
    peanut butter

¼ cup soy sauce

3 tablespoons seasoned rice vinegar

2 tablespoons lime juice

1 teaspoon liquid aminos

1 teaspoon sriracha

For the cups

1 cup bulgur

½ cup soy sauce

¼ cup seasoned rice vinegar

½ teaspoon garlic powder

½ teaspoon ground ginger

¼ teaspoon red pepper flakes

1 cup shredded carrots

1 cup shredded cabbage

½ cup sliced scallions, green and
    white parts

1 head red leaf lettuce or Bibb lettuce

To make the sauce

1. In a small bowl, combine the peanut butter, soy sauce, vinegar, lime juice, liquid aminos, and sriracha. Whisk until well combined.

To make the cups

2. In a medium saucepan, cook the bulgur according to the package instructions. Remove from the heat. Drain any excess water after cooking.

3. In a small bowl, combine the soy sauce, vinegar, garlic powder, ginger, and red pepper flakes. Mix well.

4. Add the carrots, cabbage, scallions, and soy sauce mixture to the cooked bulgur. Mix thoroughly.

5. Serve the filling scooped into individual lettuce leaves, topped with a drizzle of peanut sauce.

Ingredient Tip: Look for a brand of sriracha that doesn't have sugar listed as the second ingredient (the further back in the list sugar is, the less there is of it).

PER SERVING: Calories: 532; Fat: 17.3g; Dietary fiber: 18.1g; Protein: 24.8g; Carbohydrates: 78.8g

SPINACH SALAD WITH SWEET SMOKY DRESSING

SERVES 4 TO 6

PREP TIME: 15 MINUTES

Hot bacon dressing over hearty spinach with a pop of berry sweetness was one of my favorite steakhouse salads. But I don't miss it thanks to this WFPB version. Here, I use hearty balsamic vinegar, umami-rich soy sauce, and my secret weapon, smoked paprika, to make a bacon-like dressing.

For the dressing

¼ cup balsamic vinegar

2 tablespoons soy sauce

3 tablespoons pure maple syrup

1½ tablespoons Dijon mustard

½ teaspoon smoked paprika

For the salad

4 to 6 cups spinach

2 cups sliced strawberries

¼ red or white onion, thinly sliced and rinsed

To make the dressing

1. In a small bowl or container with a lid, combine the vinegar, soy sauce, maple syrup, mustard, and paprika. Whisk vigorously or shake.

To make the salad

2. In a large bowl, combine the spinach, strawberries, and onion.

3. Add the dressing, and toss to coat. Serve immediately.

Variation Tip: Want to up the nutrition and make this a full-on salad-for-dinner meal? Add chickpeas and a scoop of a cooked grain such as farro or quinoa when serving.

PER SERVING: Calories: 84; Fat: 0.7g; Dietary fiber: 2.6g; Protein: 2.2g; Carbohydrates: 18.4g

MLAT (MUSHROOM, LETTUCE, AVOCADO, TOMATO SANDWICH)

SERVES 4

PREP TIME: 10 MINUTES

I pair sautéed Smoky Mushrooms (page 132) with lettuce and tomato for a plant-based BLT, then take things to the next level of decadence with mashed avocado and a savory dressing on the greens. This sandwich is so good on whole-grain bread or wrapped up in a pita or grain tortilla.

8 whole-grain bread slices, toasted

1 ripe avocado, pitted, peeled, and quartered

1 batch Smoky Mushrooms (page 132)

1 to 2 cups mixed greens, lightly dressed with Sweet Smoky Dressing (page 60)

1 large tomato, sliced, or 20 to 25 grape tomatoes, sliced

1. Place 1 slice of toast on each of 4 plates, and gently mash a quarter of an avocado on each slice of toast.

2. Evenly divide and layer the mushrooms, greens, and tomatoes among the 4 sandwiches.

3. Place the remaining slices of toast on top.

Make It Even Faster: A modified version of this could be prepared with store-bought tempeh to replace the mushrooms (I recommend Lightlife's Smoky Tempeh).

PER SERVING: Calories: 181; Fat: 1.1g; Dietary fiber: 6.7g; Protein: 9.7g; Carbohydrates: 33.3g

SWEET POTATO AND BLACK BEAN QUESADILLAS

SERVES 4 TO 6

PREP TIME: 10 MINUTES | COOK TIME: 20 MINUTES

Creamy sweet potatoes and savory, spicy black beans are a perfect pair in this quick and easy quesadilla. I've found that chipotle hot sauce contributes a nice smoky finish that balances out the black bean spread. Chipotle peppers in adobo can be substituted in a pinch.

For the black bean spread

1 (15-ounce) can black beans, drained and rinsed

2 to 4 tablespoons chopped fresh cilantro stems and leaves

1 scallion, green and white parts, thinly sliced

1 tablespoon lime juice

1 teaspoon chipotle hot sauce

¼ teaspoon red miso paste

⅛ teaspoon garlic powder

For the quesadillas

1 pound sweet potatoes, peeled and shredded

4 to 6 (8-inch) whole-grain tortillas

Hot sauce or Guacamole (page 39), for serving

To make the black bean spread

1. In a small bowl, using a fork, mash the beans to a creamy texture.

2. Mix in the cilantro, scallion, lime juice, hot sauce, miso, and garlic powder.

To make the quesadillas

3. Heat a large nonstick skillet over medium heat.

4. Put the sweet potatoes in the skillet, and cook, stirring every few minutes, for about 10 minutes, or until tender and browned. Transfer to a plate.

5. Wipe out the skillet, and return to the stove.

6. Divide the bean spread (about ¼ cup to 6 tablespoons per tortilla) among the tortillas, and spread evenly.

7. Divide the sweet potatoes (about ¼ cup per tortilla) onto half of each tortilla, fold in half, and press gently.

8. Place the tortillas in the hot skillet, and cook for 2 to 5 minutes per side, or until the tortillas are golden brown. Remove from the heat.

9. Serve the quesadillas with hot sauce.

Make It Even Faster: Leftover cooked sweet potatoes can be mashed and used in place of the shredded sweet potatoes.

PER SERVING: Calories: 201; Fat: 1.1g; Dietary fiber: 6.7g; Protein: 6g; Carbohydrates: 41.2g

BAJA-STYLE TACOS

SERVES 2 TO 4

PREP TIME: 10 MINUTES | COOK TIME: 5 MINUTES

Baja-style tacos are typically made with fish or other seafood, but in this version I use Perfect Baked Tofu (page 134) as a base. You can also substitute Skillet Cauliflower Bites (page 41) for the tofu. You won't miss a thing.

½ batch Perfect Baked Tofu (page 134), warmed and cut into ½-inch dice

1 tablespoon lime juice

½ teaspoon Chili Spice Blend (page 124)

4 to 8 (4-inch) corn tortillas

1 or 2 cabbage leaves, shredded

Pico de Gallo (page 38), for serving

Guacamole (page 39), for serving

1. Line a plate with a dish towel.

2. In a small bowl, toss together the tofu, lime juice, and spice blend.

3. Warm the tortillas according to the package instructions. Transfer to the prepared plate. Fold the towel over to keep the tortillas warm until ready to serve.

4. Layer the tofu, cabbage, pico de gallo, and guacamole on the tortillas.

Make It Even Faster: Substitute salsa and sliced avocado for homemade pico de gallo and guacamole, and serve with lime wedges.

PER SERVING: Calories: 295; Fat: 9.4g; Dietary fiber: 7.4g; Protein: 6.7g; Carbohydrates: 45.4g

RAW VEGETABLE HUMMUS WRAPS

SERVES 4 TO 6

PREP TIME: 10 MINUTES | COOK TIME: 5 MINUTES

Like a salad in a tortilla, this hummus wrap is one of my favorites. Taking a bit of time to grate carrot and beet contributes a fresh juiciness to the wrap. The addition of broccoli sprouts packs a healthy punch of sulforaphane, which is known for its disease-fighting benefits.

4 to 6 (8-inch) whole-grain tortillas

1½ to 2 cups Oil-Free Hummus (page 36)

1 cup spinach or mixed baby greens

1 cup shredded beet

1 cup grated carrot

1 cup sliced red bell pepper

¼ cup broccoli sprouts

1. Warm the tortillas according to the package instructions.

2. Spread ¼ to ½ cup of hummus on each tortilla.

3. Add a small handful of spinach.

4. Top with 2 tablespoons to ¼ cup of beet, carrot, and bell pepper and about 1 tablespoon of sprouts. Wrap up the tortillas, and serve.

Variation Tip: Need a tangy boost? I sometimes like to drizzle my wrap with a bit of balsamic vinegar.

PER SERVING: Calories: 135; Fat: 1.7g; Dietary fiber: 4.7g; Protein: 5g; Carbohydrates: 25.5g

BLACK BEAN BURGERS

SERVES 4

PREP TIME: 10 MINUTES | COOK TIME: 20 MINUTES

Finally, a hearty WFPB burger that is moist when cooked yet won't fall apart. Creamy black beans and oats meld to create the perfect texture when baked. Miso and nutritional yeast round out the flavors, adding up to a rich and savory burger patty. These burgers are delicious served on a bun with all the classic fixings: lettuce, tomato, pickles, onions, mustard, and Ketchup (page 127).

1 (15-ounce) can black beans, drained and rinsed

1 cup shredded carrots

½ cup rolled oats

¼ cup hemp hearts

¼ cup nutritional yeast

1 tablespoon miso paste

1 tablespoon tahini

1 tablespoon onion powder

½ teaspoon garlic powder

½ teaspoon smoked paprika

4 whole-grain burger buns

Burger toppings of choice, for serving

1. Preheat the oven to 350°F. Line a baking sheet with parchment paper.

2. Put the beans, carrots, oats, hemp hearts, nutritional yeast, miso, tahini, onion powder, garlic powder, and paprika in a food processor. Pulse about 20 times, or until just combined (don't overdo it; the consistency should be textured).

3. Form the mixture into 4 (3-inch-diameter) ½-inch-thick patties.

4. Arrange the patties in a single layer on the prepared baking sheet.

5. Transfer the baking sheet to the oven, and bake for 10 minutes. Flip the patties, and bake for another 10 minutes, or until golden brown and the edges are slightly crispy. Remove from the oven.

6. Place the patties on the buns, and serve with your favorite burger toppings.

PER SERVING: Calories: 492; Fat: 18.3g; Dietary fiber: 15.8g; Protein: 28.4g; Carbohydrates: 57.7g

PORTABELLA MUSHROOM SANDWICHES WITH PESTO "RICOTTA"

SERVES 4

PREP TIME: 5 MINUTES | COOK TIME: 10 MINUTES

This sandwich is inspired by a messy burger I used to order at a city burger joint in my pre-WFPB days. In this recipe that's bound to become a favorite, hearty portabella mushrooms get an irresistible complement of creamy, sweet pesto "ricotta" and bright, zingy tomato sauce. With juicy, flavorful sandwiches like this, you just might not miss a burger.

¼ cup balsamic vinegar

½ teaspoon dried rosemary

¼ teaspoon garlic powder

4 portabella mushroom caps, stemmed

½ cup Tofu "Ricotta" (page 129)

¼ cup packed fresh basil, chopped

2 tablespoons nutritional yeast

2 tablespoons lemon juice

½ teaspoon garlic powder

1 cup mixed baby greens

1 cup Perfect Marinara Sauce (page 138), warmed

4 whole-grain burger buns, toasted

1. In a small bowl, mix together the vinegar, rosemary, and garlic powder.

2. Brush the mixture on the bottoms of the mushroom caps.

3. Place the mushrooms, stem-side up, in a nonstick skillet. Cover, and cook over medium heat for 3 to 5 minutes per side, or until browned and cooked, yet still plump and juicy. Remove from the heat.

4. In a small bowl, mix together the tofu ricotta, basil, nutritional yeast, lemon juice, and garlic powder.

5. Divide the tofu-basil mixture, greens, and marinara sauce among the bun bottoms.

6. Place the mushrooms, stem-side up, on top, followed by the bun tops.

Variation Tip: Can't find whole-grain burger buns? Whole-grain English muffins are a wonderful substitute.

PER SERVING: Calories: 320; Fat: 6.9g; Dietary fiber: 10g; Protein: 25.9g; Carbohydrates: 43g

Summer Vegetable Minestrone, page 78

CHAPTER 5

SOUPS AND STEWS

SOY CURL NOODLE SOUP

SERVES 4 TO 6

PREP TIME: 5 MINUTES | COOK TIME: 20 MINUTES

This comforting soup is loaded with nourishing plant-based ingredients. Soy curls are dehydrated pieces of soy. They rehydrate in liquid and have a nice chewy texture. Easily absorbing the flavors of this and other broths also makes them an extremely versatile soy ingredient to keep in the pantry.

4 cups vegetable broth

2 cups water

2 cups whole-grain rotini pasta

2 cups soy curls

1 cup frozen carrots

1 cup frozen pearl onions

¼ cup nutritional yeast

1 teaspoon dried rosemary

½ teaspoon freshly ground black pepper

1. In a large Dutch oven or saucepan, combine the broth, water, pasta, soy curls, carrots, onions, nutritional yeast, rosemary, and pepper. Bring to a boil over high heat.

2. Reduce the heat to low. Cover, and simmer for 10 to 15 minutes, or until the pasta is tender. Remove from the heat. Serve immediately.

PER SERVING: Calories: 195; Fat: 4g; Dietary fiber: 6.5g; Protein: 14.6g; Carbohydrates: 26.5g

MISO NOODLE SOUP WITH SHIITAKE MUSHROOMS

SERVES 4 TO 6

PREP TIME: 5 MINUTES | COOK TIME: 25 MINUTES

This delicious noodle soup with an Asian-inspired flair makes for an enjoyable, healthy, and quick weeknight meal that's faster than takeout. I use shiitake mushrooms to achieve a savory, umami-rich broth, which is further enhanced by the addition of miso paste and soy sauce.

1 (8-ounce) package brown rice noodles

4 cups vegetable broth

2 cups water

1 (5-ounce) package shiitake mushrooms, cut into ¼-inch-thick slices

3 scallions, green and white parts, thinly sliced on a bias (about ½ cup)

3 garlic cloves, sliced

3 or 4 (¼-inch) slices unpeeled fresh ginger

8 ounces bok choy

2 tablespoons red miso paste

1 tablespoon soy sauce

1. Cook the noodles according to the package instructions.

2. Meanwhile, in a large Dutch oven or saucepan, combine the broth, water, mushrooms, scallions, garlic, and ginger. Cover, and bring to a boil over high heat.

3. Reduce the heat to low. Cover, and simmer for 15 minutes.

4. Uncover, and increase the heat to medium. Add the bok choy, and simmer for 3 minutes, or until the bok choy is crisp-tender.

5. Add the noodles, and heat through. Remove from the heat.

6. Add the miso and soy sauce. Stir until the miso has dissolved.

7. Remove the ginger, and serve.

Variation Tip: If you prefer a spicy soup, add thinly sliced fresh chiles or jalapeños when you add the ginger in step 2.

PER SERVING: Calories: 396; Fat: 3.3g; Dietary fiber: 8.1g; Protein: 12.7g; Carbohydrates: 80g

WEEKNIGHT TOMATO SOUP

SERVES 4

PREP TIME: 5 MINUTES | COOK TIME: 25 MINUTES

This soup is as simple as can be. Open a couple cans, measure a few spices and herbs, and voilà, you have a delicious tomato soup that also happens to be oil-free with no added salt. Pair it with the Sweet Potato and Black Bean Quesadillas (page 62) or a simple salad for the perfect easy weeknight dinner.

1 (28-ounce) can crushed tomatoes in puree

1 cup vegetable broth

2 tablespoons nutritional yeast

1 tablespoon onion powder

1 teaspoon paprika

¼ teaspoon garlic powder

¼ teaspoon freshly ground black pepper

⅛ teaspoon cayenne

1. In a medium saucepan, stir together the tomatoes, broth, nutritional yeast, onion powder, paprika, garlic powder, pepper, and cayenne. Bring to a simmer over medium-high heat.

2. Reduce the heat to low. Cover, and simmer for 15 to 20 minutes, or until the flavors have melded. Remove from the heat. Serve immediately.

Variation Tip: Homemade croutons make for a nice addition to this soup. Cut up whole-grain bread and then mix with a tablespoon of Sweet Smoky Dressing (page 60). Spread evenly on a parchment paper–lined baking sheet, and transfer to a cold oven. Set the temperature to 350°F. Once the oven reaches temperature, cook, stirring occasionally to avoid burning, for 10 to 15 minutes, or until the croutons are dried and toasted.

PER SERVING: Calories: 93; Fat: 0.4g; Dietary fiber: 4.1g; Protein: 6.2g; Carbohydrates: 16.1g

BLACK BEAN SOUP

SERVES 4 TO 6

PREP TIME: 5 MINUTES | COOK TIME: 25 MINUTES

This filling black bean soup makes an excellent dinner on a brisk fall day or any other time you need to fuel up. Fire-roasted tomatoes add a rich, smoky flavor that is boosted by the addition of smoked paprika. Black beans are high in protein and fiber and boast a balance of minerals and nutrients that provide many health benefits.

2 (14-ounce) cans black beans, including liquid

1 (14-ounce) can fire-roasted diced tomatoes

1 (8-ounce) can salsa verde

1 cup vegetable broth

½ cup frozen corn

1 tablespoon chipotle hot sauce (or chipotle in adobo)

1 tablespoon onion powder

1 teaspoon ground cumin

1 teaspoon smoked paprika

½ teaspoon garlic powder

1 bay leaf

1. In a large Dutch oven or saucepan, combine the beans, tomatoes, salsa, broth, corn, hot sauce, onion powder, cumin, paprika, garlic powder, and bay leaf. Bring to a boil over high heat.

2. Reduce the heat to low. Cover, and simmer for 15 to 20 minutes, or until the soup is cooked and flavors have melded together. Remove from the heat.

3. Remove the bay leaf, and serve.

PER SERVING: Calories: 126; Fat: 1.1g; Dietary fiber: 5.4g; Protein: 7g; Carbohydrates: 24.5g

WHITE JACKFRUIT CHILI

SERVES 6 TO 8

PREP TIME: 5 MINUTES | COOK TIME: 25 MINUTES

Inspired by white chicken chili recipes, I use shredded jackfruit to get a similar texture. Canned young jackfruit can be found at many grocery stores and Asian markets. Fresh ripe jackfruit would be too sweet for this type of savory recipe. I use a salsa verde in this recipe to balance the flavors, so look for one with simple plant-based ingredients.

3 cups vegetable broth

1 (15-ounce) can young jackfruit, drained, shredded, and rinsed

1 (15-ounce) can white beans, drained and rinsed

1 (15-ounce) can pinto beans, drained and rinsed

1 (15-ounce) can hominy, drained and rinsed

2 (4-ounce) cans green chiles

1 cup salsa verde

1 tablespoon onion powder

2 teaspoons ground cumin

½ teaspoon ground coriander

½ teaspoon garlic powder

3 scallions, green and white parts, thinly sliced

½ cup packed fresh cilantro, minced

1 tablespoon lime juice

1. In a large Dutch oven or saucepan, combine the broth, jackfruit, white beans, pinto beans, hominy, chiles, salsa, onion powder, cumin, coriander, and garlic powder. Bring to a boil over high heat.

2. Reduce the heat to medium-low. Simmer for 15 to 20 minutes, or until the chili is cooked and flavors have melded together. Remove from the heat.

3. Stir in the scallions, cilantro, and lime juice. Serve immediately.

Ingredient Tip: To prepare jackfruit, drain it and then shred by pulling it apart with your fingers to break up large pieces and seed pods. Then rinse it very well. To make the process easy, I shred it in a colander and then rinse it thoroughly.

PER SERVING: Calories: 201; Fat: 1.6g; Dietary fiber: 6g; Protein: 7.4g; Carbohydrates: 43.1g

BEAN AND BULGUR CHILI

SERVES 4 TO 6

PREP TIME: 5 MINUTES | COOK TIME: 25 MINUTES

This quick chili is packed with flavor thanks to fire-roasted tomatoes and piquant herbs and spices. Using bulgur provides a "meat-like" texture while packing in vitamins, nutrients, and fiber. Serve it with Quick Spelt Bread (page 136) or oil-free Tortilla Chips (page 33) and Guacamole (page 39). Another tasty meal idea: serve this chili over Potato Wedges (page 135), and top it with the queso from the Potato Queso Bowl (page 96).

1 (28-ounce) can crushed fire-roasted tomatoes

1 (15-ounce) can kidney beans, drained and rinsed

1 (15-ounce) can pinto beans, drained and rinsed

1 (14-ounce) can diced fire-roasted tomatoes

1 (4-ounce) can green chiles

½ cup medium-grind red bulgur

½ cup vegetable broth or water

2 tablespoons chili powder

1 tablespoon onion powder

1 teaspoon paprika

1 teaspoon ground cumin

½ teaspoon garlic powder

½ teaspoon dried oregano

¼ teaspoon freshly ground black pepper

⅛ teaspoon cayenne

¼ cup lime juice

½ cup packed fresh cilantro, chopped

1. In a large Dutch oven or saucepan, combine the crushed tomatoes, kidney beans, pinto beans, diced tomatoes, chiles, bulgur, broth, chili powder, onion powder, paprika, cumin, garlic powder, oregano, pepper, and cayenne. Bring to a boil over high heat.

2. Reduce the heat to low. Cover, and simmer, stirring occasionally, for 20 to 25 minutes, or until the chili is fragrant and cooked through. Remove from the heat.

3. Stir in the lime juice and cilantro. Serve immediately.

PER SERVING: Calories: 254; Fat: 2.4g; Dietary fiber: 16.1g; Protein: 9.8g; Carbohydrates: 53.7g

SUMMER VEGETABLE MINESTRONE

SERVES 4 TO 6
PREP TIME: 5 MINUTES | COOK TIME: 25 MINUTES

This tasty minestrone is light and fresh, just what you desire in a summer soup. I love to make it when fresh zucchini and basil are available at the farmers' market. It pairs well with Hemp Heart "Parmesan" (page 125) and Quick Spelt Bread (page 136).

2 celery stalks, thinly sliced
(about 1 cup)

1 shallot, thinly sliced (about 1 cup)

3 garlic cloves, sliced or minced

¼ cup water

3 cups vegetable broth

2 small zucchini, halved and cut into
¼-inch-thick slices (about 2 cups)

2 small yellow squash, halved and
cut into ¼-inch-thick slices
(about 2 cups)

1 (28-ounce) can crushed tomatoes
with basil

1 (15-ounce) can Great Northern beans

4 ounces whole-grain rotini pasta
(about 2 cups)

1 cup loosely packed fresh
basil, chopped

1. In a Dutch oven or saucepan, combine the celery, shallot, garlic, and water. Sauté over medium heat for about 5 minutes, or until soft.

2. Add the broth, zucchini, squash, tomatoes, and beans with their liquid. Cover, and bring to a boil over high heat.

3. Reduce the heat to a medium-low. Simmer for about 5 minutes.

4. Stir in the pasta, cover, and simmer, stirring occasionally, for about 10 minutes, or until the pasta is tender. Remove from the heat.

5. Stir in the basil, and serve.

Ingredient Tip: I use an equal mix of zucchini and summer squash, but this could be made with any combination of zucchini and squash or just one or the other.

PER SERVING: Calories: 265; Fat: 1g; Dietary fiber: 10.4g; Protein: 13g; Carbohydrates: 54.5g

POTATO, CARROT, AND MUSHROOM STEW

SERVES 4 TO 6

PREP TIME: 5 MINUTES | COOK TIME: 25 MINUTES

This "beefy" stew always brings back nostalgic memories from my childhood. I remember my mom making a beef noodle stew, and this recipe re-creates that flavor and texture with WFPB ingredients. To achieve a similar depth of flavor, I use dried porcini mushrooms and tomato paste, each of which adds a savory richness to this stew.

4 cups vegetable broth

1½ pounds yellow potatoes, cut into ½-inch dice (about 4 cups)

1 cup frozen carrots

1 cup frozen pearl onions

2 tablespoons tomato paste

3 strips dried porcini mushrooms, chopped (about 2 tablespoons)

1 tablespoon onion powder

½ teaspoon dried thyme

¼ teaspoon garlic powder

1 bay leaf

½ cup frozen peas

2 tablespoons red miso paste

1 tablespoon balsamic vinegar

1. In a large Dutch oven or saucepan, combine the broth, potatoes, carrots, onions, tomato paste, mushrooms, onion powder, thyme, garlic powder, and bay leaf. Bring to a boil over high heat.

2. Reduce the heat to low. Cover, and simmer for 15 minutes, or until the potatoes are tender and a knife slides in easily. Remove from the heat.

3. Add the peas, miso, and vinegar. Stir until the miso has dissolved.

4. Remove the bay leaf, and serve immediately.

Variation Tip: Serve over whole-grain rotini pasta to enjoy this dish "stroganoff"-style.

PER SERVING: Calories: 183; Fat: 1.3g; Dietary fiber: 4.9g; Protein: 8.3g; Carbohydrates: 35.9g

SAVORY PUMPKIN BISQUE

SERVES 4

PREP TIME: 5 MINUTES | COOK TIME: 20 MINUTES

Inspired by light aromatic flavors, this pumpkin soup with its savory-buttery notes is a cozy and filling meal on a chilly fall day. Soy sauce adds a depth of umami flavor to balance out the sweet pumpkin and maple syrup. I like to use plain pumpkin puree, not pumpkin pie filling (which often has sugar and other ingredients already mixed in), so I can control the flavor of the soup.

2 (15-ounce) cans pumpkin puree

3 cups vegetable broth

2 tablespoons nutritional yeast

2 tablespoons apple cider vinegar

1 tablespoon onion powder

1 tablespoon soy sauce

2 teaspoons pure maple syrup

½ teaspoon dried thyme

½ teaspoon freshly ground black pepper

¼ teaspoon garlic powder

2 bay leaves

1. In a Dutch oven or saucepan, combine the pumpkin puree, broth, nutritional yeast, vinegar, onion powder, soy sauce, maple syrup, thyme, pepper, garlic powder, and bay leaves. Bring to a simmer over medium-high heat. Cover, and cook for 20 minutes, or until the soup is fragrant and heated through. Remove from the heat.

2. Remove the bay leaves, and serve.

PER SERVING: Calories: 133; Fat: 2g; Dietary fiber: 7.8g; Protein: 8.6g; Carbohydrates: 23.4g

LENTIL SOUP

SERVES 2 TO 4

PREP TIME: 5 MINUTES | COOK TIME: 25 MINUTES

Lentils are packed with nutrients that keep our bodies running smoothly. High in antioxidants, protein, fiber, iron, and potassium, they can reduce the risk of heart disease, help repair cell walls, and improve digestion. This is why they should be a staple in your WFPB diet. This light, smoky, and aromatic soup is a perfect way to ensure those essential nutrients are part of your meal plan.

4 cups vegetable broth

1 cup dried green or brown lentils, rinsed

2 teaspoon onion powder

1 teaspoon dried parsley

½ teaspoon ground cumin

½ teaspoon smoked paprika

¼ teaspoon garlic powder

¼ teaspoon ground coriander

1 bay leaf

1. In a Dutch oven or saucepan, combine the broth, lentils, onion powder, parsley, cumin, paprika, garlic powder, coriander, and bay leaf. Bring to a boil over high heat.

2. Reduce the heat to medium-low. Cover, and simmer for 20 minutes, or until the lentils are tender. Remove from the heat.

3. Remove the bay leaf, and serve immediately.

PER SERVING: Calories: 100; Fat: 3.1g; Dietary fiber: 1.4g; Protein: 10.6g; Carbohydrates: 6.8g

CREAMY CORN CHOWDER

SERVES 4 TO 6

PREP TIME: 5 MINUTES | COOK TIME: 25 MINUTES

Blending the corn provides texture to this creamy, hearty chowder and also helps distribute the flavor of the corn throughout the broth. Colorful mixed vegetables, like carrots, peas, and green beans, add extra flavor, textures, and nutrients to round out the soup. I like to make this soup on a Sunday and pack it in microwavable bowls for quick and hearty grab-and-go lunches during the week.

2 cups vegetable broth

1½ cups frozen corn

1 cup unsweetened soy milk

½ cup chopped celery (about 1 stalk)

4 cups diced yellow potatoes

1 cup frozen mixed vegetables

2 tablespoons nutritional yeast

1 tablespoon onion powder

1 tablespoon liquid aminos

½ teaspoon smoked paprika

¼ teaspoon freshly ground black pepper

¼ teaspoon dried thyme

¼ teaspoon garlic powder

2 tablespoons red-wine vinegar

1. In a blender, combine the broth, corn, soy milk, and celery. Process until smooth.

2. Transfer to a Dutch oven or saucepan.

3. Add the potatoes, mixed vegetables, nutritional yeast, onion powder, liquid aminos, paprika, pepper, thyme, and garlic powder. Partially cover, and bring to a simmer over high heat.

4. Reduce the heat to medium-low. Simmer for 20 minutes, or until the potatoes are tender and a knife slides in easily. Remove from the heat.

5. Stir in the vinegar, and serve.

PER SERVING: Calories: 211; Fat: 2.4g; Dietary fiber: 7.4g; Protein: 10.4g; Carbohydrates: 39.4g

VEGETABLE GOULASH

SERVES 4 TO 6

PREP TIME: 5 MINUTES | COOK TIME: 25 MINUTES

Light and peppery, this WFPB-style goulash is reminiscent of a roasted red pepper bisque, only with an unblended broth. The sweet paprika provides a delicate flavor while the smoked paprika, roasted red pepper, tomato paste, and dried porcini mushrooms add depth. The addition of potatoes creates a balanced and hearty stew.

4 cups vegetable broth

4 cups diced (½-inch) yellow potatoes

2 cups frozen carrots

2 tablespoons tomato paste

½ cup chopped water-packed roasted red pepper

¼ cup sweet paprika

1 teaspoon whole caraway seeds

3 strips dried porcini mushrooms, chopped (about 2 tablespoons)

1 tablespoon onion powder

½ teaspoon garlic powder

2 teaspoons dried parsley

½ teaspoon smoked paprika

1 bay leaf

1. In a large Dutch oven or saucepan, combine the broth, potatoes, carrots, tomato paste, roasted red pepper, sweet paprika, caraway, mushrooms, onion powder, garlic powder, parsley, smoked paprika, and bay leaf. Bring to a boil over high heat.

2. Reduce the heat to low. Cover, and simmer for 15 to 20 minutes, or until the potatoes are tender and a knife slides in easily. Remove from the heat.

3. Remove the bay leaf, and serve.

PER SERVING: Calories: 295; Fat: 2.4g; Dietary fiber: 10.2g; Protein: 14.2g; Carbohydrates: 55.3g

Broccoli and Mushroom Stir-Fry, page 98

MAINS

QUINOA SUPER BOWL

SERVES 6
PREP TIME: 20 MINUTES

In addition to loads of vegetables; grains; and a bright lemon, thyme, and tahini dressing, this bowl gets an elevated texture twist with a carrot-cashew pâté.

For the pâté

1 cup raw cashews

1 cup chopped carrots

2 tablespoons red miso paste

2 tablespoons lemon juice

For the dressing

½ cup tahini

6 tablespoons water

6 tablespoons lemon juice

½ teaspoon dried thyme

¼ teaspoon garlic powder

4 teaspoons seasoned rice vinegar

For the quinoa bowl

4 cups cooked quinoa

2 cups bite-size cauliflower florets

4 cups fresh baby spinach

1 (15-ounce) can chickpeas, drained and rinsed

2 cups cooked beets

Freshly ground black pepper

To make the pâté

1. In a food processor, combine the cashews, carrots, miso, and lemon juice. Process until smooth.

To make the dressing

2. In a small bowl, whisk together the tahini, water, lemon juice, thyme, garlic powder, and vinegar.

To make the quinoa bowl

3. Divide the quinoa, cauliflower, spinach, chickpeas, and beets among 4 large plates.

4. Add 2 tablespoons of the pâté and 3 to 4 tablespoons of the dressing. Season with pepper, and serve.

PER SERVING (¼ CUP): Calories: 327; Fat: 22.2g; Dietary fiber: 6.4g; Protein: 10.7g; Carbohydrates: 25.5g

LENTIL BOLOGNESE

SERVES 4 TO 6

PREP TIME: 5 MINUTES | COOK TIME: 25 MINUTES

Rich and reminiscent of Sunday family dinners, this hearty sauce cooks in 30 minutes but tastes like it's been cooking all day. I use dried porcini mushrooms for their depth of flavor and fresh vegetables to bring out the earthy, sweet notes. Serve this with your favorite pasta.

3 medium celery stalks, diced
(about 1 cup)

2 medium carrots, diced (about 1 cup)

1 small onion, diced (about 1 cup)

1 cup vegetable broth

½ cup dried green lentils

2 dried porcini mushrooms, chopped

1 cup water

1 cup Perfect Marinara Sauce
(page 138)

2 teaspoons soy sauce

¼ cup Tofu "Ricotta" (page 129)

1 teaspoon red-wine vinegar

1. In a saucepan, combine the celery, carrots, onion, and broth. Cover, and sweat over low heat for about 5 minutes, or until the vegetables are soft.

2. Add the lentils, mushrooms, and water.

3. Increase the heat to medium-low. Cover, and simmer for 20 minutes, or until the lentils are soft.

4. Stir in the marinara sauce and soy sauce. Heat through. Remove from the heat.

5. Stir in the tofu ricotta and vinegar, and serve.

Make It Even Faster: In a time crunch? You can use 1 cup of your favorite store-bought oil-free, WFPB pasta sauce.

PER SERVING (¼ CUP): Calories: 136; Fat: 0.5g; Dietary fiber: 9.1g; Protein: 7.8g; Carbohydrates: 25.1g (without pasta or grain)

ENCHILADAS

SERVES 2 TO 4

PREP TIME: 10 MINUTES | COOK TIME: 20 MINUTES

Casserole-style meals are a perennial comfort food favorite, but they are often laden with high-fat animal products. You'll be pleased with these satisfying enchiladas, which pair a tasty WFPB-approved filling with a rich, spiced tomato-based sauce. Using canned potatoes brings this dish together in 30 minutes, making it perfect for a weeknight meal. Serve with crisp, shredded cabbage and creamy avocado to balance out the dish.

For the enchilada sauce

1 (15-ounce) can no-salt-added tomato sauce

2 tablespoons seasoned rice vinegar

2 tablespoons apple cider vinegar

1 tablespoon chili powder

2 teaspoons paprika

1 teaspoon onion powder

1 teaspoon chipotle hot sauce

1 teaspoon pure maple syrup

½ teaspoon garlic powder

½ teaspoon ground cumin

¼ teaspoon ground coriander

¼ teaspoon freshly ground black pepper

To make the enchilada sauce

1. In a small bowl, whisk together the tomato sauce, rice vinegar, cider vinegar, chili powder, paprika, onion powder, hot sauce, maple syrup, garlic powder, cumin, coriander, and pepper.

To make the enchiladas

2. Preheat the oven to 350°F.

3. To make the filling, in a medium bowl, stir together the potatoes, chiles, beans, onion powder, garlic powder, and cumin.

4. Spread ½ cup of the enchilada sauce over the bottom of an 8-by-8-inch glass baking dish.

For the enchiladas

1 (15-ounce) can new potatoes, drained and diced

1 (4-ounce) can green chiles, drained

½ cup canned black beans, drained and rinsed

1 teaspoon onion powder

½ teaspoon garlic powder

½ teaspoon ground cumin

8 (4-inch) corn tortillas

½ cup thinly shredded red or green cabbage

1 lime, cut into wedges

Ripe avocado, pitted, peeled, and sliced or mashed, for serving (optional)

5. Lay 1 tortilla on a flat surface, and spoon in about 2 heaping tablespoons of enchilada filling. Gently roll the tortilla up, and place in the baking dish, seam-side down. Repeat for the rest of the tortillas, laying them side by side until the dish is full. (You may need to squeeze them in or lay some the opposite way to fit them all in.)

6. Cover the filled enchiladas with the remaining enchilada sauce. Cover the baking dish with aluminum foil.

7. Bake for 20 minutes. Remove from the oven. Let stand for 5 minutes.

8. Serve the enchiladas with the cabbage, lime, and avocado (if using).

Ingredient Tip: Prefer to use fresh potatoes? Simply boil yellow potatoes until tender, let them cool until they are cool enough to touch, dice, and replace in the recipe. You will need about 1½ cups diced potatoes.

PER SERVING: Calories: 283; Fat: 10.7g; Dietary fiber: 11.7g; Protein: 7.7g; Carbohydrates: 44.6g

FREEKEH PIZZA SKILLET

SERVES 4 TO 6

PREP TIME: 5 MINUTES | COOK TIME: 30 MINUTES

Who doesn't love the flavors of rich tomato sauce and creamy ricotta? This skillet meal brings them together in a layered cooking method to steam the kale and heat the sauce without jeopardizing the cooking time of the freekeh. Freekeh is a cracked wheat product that offers both high protein and fiber. It has a nutty and slightly wheat-like flavor, which is complimentary to the rich tomato sauce in this pasta-inspired dish.

8 ounces sliced cremini mushrooms

2 tablespoons water, plus
    2 cups, divided

1 cup freekeh

1 tablespoon onion powder

¼ teaspoon garlic powder

3 cups shredded curly kale

2 cups Perfect Marinara Sauce
    (page 138)

½ to 1 cup Tofu "Ricotta" (page 129)

1. In a sauté pan or skillet, combine the mushrooms and 2 tablespoons of water. Cook over medium heat for 4 to 10 minutes, or until browned.

2. Add the freekeh, remaining 2 cups of water, the onion powder, and garlic powder. Stir to combine.

3. Add the kale on top of the freekeh mixture to steam. Do not stir.

4. Reduce the heat to low. Cover, and simmer for 10 minutes.

5. Layer the marinara sauce on top of the kale. Cover, and simmer for another 10 minutes. Remove from the heat. Let sit for 5 minutes, then stir the layers together.

6. Serve the skillet with 2 to 3 tablespoons of tofu ricotta per serving.

Pair It With: Add a sprinkle of Hemp Heart "Parmesan" (page 125) for an even richer taste.

PER SERVING: Calories: 224; Fat: 2.1g; Dietary fiber: 7.2g; Protein: 11.6g; Carbohydrates: 42.1g

PASTA CARBONARA

SERVES 6

PREP TIME: 5 MINUTES | COOK TIME: 25 MINUTES

Inspired by the traditional egg-and-bacon carbonara, I created a lighter, WFPB-friendly version that combines a creamy tofu mixture with Smoky Mushrooms (page 132). I typically serve it over spaghetti or linguine, but it would also work well with a curly pasta like rotini.

1 pound whole-grain pasta

8 ounces silken tofu

½ cup unsweetened soy milk

2 tablespoons chickpea flour

6 tablespoons nutritional yeast, divided

1 tablespoon lemon juice

2 teaspoons liquid aminos

1 teaspoon onion powder

½ teaspoon garlic powder

1 teaspoon dried parsley

½ teaspoon freshly ground black pepper

1 cup Smoky Mushrooms (page 132)

½ cup frozen peas, thawed for 10 minutes

Hemp Heart "Parmesan" (page 125), for garnish

1. Cook the pasta according to the package instructions. Remove from the heat. Reserve ½ cup of the cooking water, then drain the pasta.

2. Meanwhile, to make the tofu cream, combine the tofu, soy milk, chickpea flour, 4 tablespoons of nutritional yeast, the lemon juice, liquid aminos, onion powder, and garlic powder in a blender. Process until smooth.

3. In a sauté pan or skillet, combine the tofu cream with the parsley, pepper, and ¼ cup of the pasta cooking water. Bring to a simmer over medium-low heat. Cook for about 5 minutes, or until the sauce is slightly thickened and silky.

4. Add the mushrooms and peas. Heat through. Remove from the heat.

5. Fold in the cooked pasta and remaining 2 tablespoons of nutritional yeast, adding the remaining pasta cooking water, 1 tablespoon at a time (up to ¼ cup), as needed to loosen the sauce and make tossing easier.

6. Garnish with Hemp Heart "Parmesan." Serve immediately.

Leftovers Tip: If you plan on having leftovers, save an extra ½ cup of the pasta cooking water, and stir it into leftovers, 1 tablespoon at a time, to loosen the pasta before storing.

PER SERVING: Calories: 312; Fat: 3.8g; Dietary fiber: 3.7g; Protein: 18.1g; Carbohydrates: 52g

SLOPPY JOES

SERVES 4 TO 6

PREP TIME: 5 MINUTES | COOK TIME: 20 MINUTES

By using a small grain like bulgur, you can achieve a sloppy joe's meaty texture with only whole-food, plant-based ingredients. Bulgur absorbs the flavor of the sauce, while the beans contribute to the complex texture. To make a complete meal, I like to serve these with Spinach Salad with Sweet Smoky Dressing (page 60) or Potato Wedges (page 135).

1 (15-ounce) can no-salt-added tomato sauce

2 tablespoons blackstrap molasses

2 tablespoons yellow mustard

1 tablespoon vegan Worcestershire sauce

1 tablespoon apple cider vinegar

1 tablespoon onion powder

1 teaspoon freshly ground black pepper

1 teaspoon liquid aminos

1 teaspoon chili powder

½ teaspoon garlic powder

½ cup water

½ cup medium-grind bulgur

1 (15-ounce) can pinto beans, drained and rinsed

4 to 6 whole-grain buns, toasted

1. In a medium saucepan, mix together the tomato sauce, molasses, mustard, Worcestershire sauce, vinegar, onion powder, pepper, liquid aminos, chili powder, and garlic powder.

2. Add the water, bulgur, and beans. Cover, and simmer over medium-low heat, stirring occasionally, for about 20 minutes, or until the bulgur is tender. Remove from the heat.

3. Serve the mixture on the buns.

Ingredient Tip: Worcestershire sauce usually contains anchovies, but I have found vegan Worcestershire at many grocery stores. However, if you can't find it, you can substitute Pickapeppa Sauce (original flavor).

PER SERVING: Calories: 210; Fat: 2.7g; Dietary fiber: 7.3g; Protein: 8.1g; Carbohydrates: 40.2g

BARBECUE JACKFRUIT SANDWICHES

SERVES 6 TO 8

PREP TIME: 5 MINUTES | COOK TIME: 25 MINUTES

Tender jackfruit simmered in a sweet and smoky sauce will remind you of classic barbecue. You can easily make these sandwiches as a weeknight meal for two by halving the recipe. Or increase it and make it for the crowd at your next potluck or party.

For the jackfruit

2 (15-ounce) cans young jackfruit, drained, shredded, and rinsed (see recipe tip for White Jackfruit Chili on page 76)

2 cups Homemade Barbecue Sauce (page 126)

For the coleslaw

1 cup shredded red or green cabbage

2 tablespoons seasoned rice vinegar

For the sandwiches

6 to 8 whole-grain buns or English muffins

Dill pickles, for topping (optional)

To make the jackfruit

1. In a sauté pan or skillet, combine the jackfruit and sauce. Cover, and simmer over medium-low heat for about 15 minutes.

2. Uncover, and simmer for 5 to 10 minutes, or until the jackfruit mixture is sticky to your liking. Remove from the heat.

To make the coleslaw

3. While the jackfruit cooks, in a small bowl, mix together the cabbage and vinegar.

To make the sandwiches

4. Stuff the buns with the jackfruit, coleslaw, and pickles (if using) and serve.

Variation Tip: These work great as sliders if you can find whole-grain slider buns.

PER SERVING: Calories: 166; Fat: 0.6g; Dietary fiber: 7.1g; Protein: 3g; Carbohydrates: 26.7g

POTATO QUESO BOWL

SERVES 4
PREP TIME: 5 MINUTES | COOK TIME: 25 MINUTES

When I was transitioning to a whole-food, plant-based way of eating, I made this recipe at least twice a week. I prefer to use potatoes that are an inch in diameter for a faster cooking time (usually ready in 10 minutes), but any size potato will do; you will simply need to adjust your cooking time.

2 pounds small yellow potatoes

1 cup cooked butternut squash

½ cup medium salsa

½ cup water

¼ cup raw cashews

¼ cup nutritional yeast

1 teaspoon red miso paste

⅛ teaspoon smoked paprika

1 (15-ounce) can black beans, drained, rinsed, and heated

1 to 2 cups cooked broccoli

1. Put the potatoes in a large saucepan, and add enough water to cover the potatoes by 1 inch. Bring to a boil over high heat.

2. Reduce the heat to medium. Cover, and cook for 10 to 20 minutes, or until a paring knife slides easily into a potato. Remove from the heat. Drain.

3. While the potatoes cook, combine the squash, salsa, water, cashews, nutritional yeast, miso, and paprika in a high-efficiency blender. Blend until smooth.

4. Divide the potatoes among 4 bowls. Top with the beans, broccoli, and the squash "queso."

Ingredient Tip: You can use frozen butternut squash instead, which is ready in minutes in the microwave.

PER SERVING: Calories: 321; Fat: 5.3g; Dietary fiber: 10.2g; Protein: 13.8g; Carbohydrates: 58.3g

BROWN RICE NOODLE BOWL

SERVES 2 TO 4

PREP TIME: 10 MINUTES | COOK TIME: 10 MINUTES

I like to use brown rice noodles for this dish, but a whole-grain linguine or spaghetti would work as well. When I am watching the quantity of high-fat WFPB foods I am eating, I opt for a quarter of an avocado per serving instead of half.

1 (8-ounce) package brown rice noodles

½ cup soy sauce

¼ cup seasoned rice vinegar

1 tablespoon pure maple syrup

½ teaspoon ground ginger

½ teaspoon garlic powder

⅛ teaspoon red pepper flakes

1 cup shredded carrot

2 cups shredded red cabbage

3 scallions, green and white parts, thinly sliced (about ½ cup)

½ cup loosely packed fresh cilantro, chopped

½ cup edamame, cooked

½ batch Perfect Baked Tofu (page 134) (optional)

1 ripe avocado, pitted, peeled, and sliced (optional)

1 tablespoon sesame seeds, toasted

1. Cook the noodles according to the package instructions (usually a 5 minute soak in boiled water). Drain, and rinse in cool water. Set aside to cool.

2. In a small bowl, whisk together the soy sauce, vinegar, maple syrup, ginger, garlic powder, and red pepper flakes.

3. In a large bowl, combine the noodles, carrot, cabbage, scallions, cilantro, edamame, and tofu (if using).

4. Pour the soy sauce mixture into the large bowl, and toss.

5. Top with the avocado (if using) and sesame seeds. Serve at room temperature.

Ingredient Tip: To toast sesame seeds, heat a small skillet over low heat, and pour in 1 tablespoon sesame seeds. Toast, constantly shaking the pan to prevent burning, for 5 to 7 minutes, or until the seeds are browned and fragrant. Remove from the heat. Transfer to a small bowl.

PER SERVING: Calories: 496; Fat: 18.4g; Dietary fiber: 12.2g; Protein: 20.7g; Carbohydrates: 67.5g

BROCCOLI AND MUSHROOM STIR-FRY

SERVES 4

PREP TIME: 5 MINUTES | COOK TIME: 25 MINUTES

Cooking for meat eaters has its challenges, especially if they are picky eaters. During a visit with my brother, I created this dish inspired by his love of mushrooms. He had two servings, so I'd say that it was a success! The recipe keeps it simple with carrots, broccoli, and mushrooms, but you could mix it up with a variety of vegetables. It's tasty and faster than takeout.

¼ cup soy sauce

¼ cup water, plus
    5 tablespoons, divided

2 tablespoons seasoned rice vinegar

½ teaspoon garlic powder

¼ teaspoon ground ginger

¼ to ½ teaspoon red pepper flakes

2 teaspoons cornstarch

2 (8-ounce) containers sliced
    cremini mushrooms

3 scallions, green and white parts, thinly
    sliced (about ½ cup)

1 cup sliced (¼-inch-thick) carrots

3 cups (1-inch) broccoli florets

4 to 6 cups cooked brown rice

Sesame seeds, for garnish

1. In a small bowl, whisk together the soy sauce, ¼ cup of water, the vinegar, garlic powder, ginger, red pepper flakes, and cornstarch.

2. In a large sauté pan or skillet, combine the mushrooms, scallions, and 1 tablespoon of water. Sauté over high heat, stirring occasionally, for about 10 minutes, or until the mushrooms have browned and most of the liquid has evaporated. Transfer to a dish.

3. Return the pan to the stove. Still over high heat, add the carrots and 2 tablespoons of water. Cook, stirring occasionally, for 3 minutes, or until slightly softened.

4. Stir in the broccoli and remaining 2 tablespoons of water. Cook (adding a tablespoon of water as necessary to prevent burning) for about 6 minutes, or until the broccoli is bright green and crisp-tender and the liquid has evaporated.

5. Return the mushrooms with their liquid to the pan.

6. Stir in the soy sauce mixture, and cook for 1 to 2 minutes, or until the sauce thickens. Remove from the heat.

7. Serve the stir-fry over the brown rice, and garnish with sesame seeds.

Ingredient Tip: I add 1 tablespoon water with the mushrooms to prevent them from sticking to the pan and to get the cooking started. I keep a little cup of water next to the pan to add a tablespoon at time as needed to prevent burning. Mushrooms are a high-water ingredient, so additional water may not be needed, but you should keep the water nearby when cooking the broccoli. If you'd rather use fresh ginger and garlic, use about 1 tablespoon minced or grated ginger and 3 minced garlic cloves with the mushrooms and scallions.

PER SERVING: Calories: 364; Fat: 3.4g; Dietary fiber: 4.5g; Protein: 11g; Carbohydrates: 73g

BEANS AND GREENS SKILLET DINNER

SERVES 6 TO 8
PREP TIME: 10 MINUTES | COOK TIME: 20 MINUTES

Traditional Italian-style beans and greens use sausages and oil, neither of which is WFPB approved. To achieve a flavorful beans and greens skillet dinner, I use vegetable broth, nutritional yeast, fire-roasted tomatoes, and smoked paprika. The combination of these flavors and the extra garlic give this dish a deep flavor.

2 cups vegetable broth

1 (28-ounce) can crushed fire-roasted tomatoes

2 (15-ounce) cans Great Northern beans, drained and rinsed

1 cup quinoa, rinsed

1 tablespoon nutritional yeast

1 teaspoon garlic powder

½ teaspoon red pepper flakes

¼ teaspoon smoked paprika

1 bay leaf

¼ teaspoon freshly ground black pepper

1 bunch curly kale, stemmed

Hemp Heart "Parmesan" (page 125), for garnish

1. In a Dutch oven or saucepan, combine the broth, tomatoes, beans, quinoa, nutritional yeast, garlic powder, red pepper flakes, paprika, bay leaf, and pepper. Bring to a boil over high heat.

2. Reduce the heat to medium-low. Cover, and simmer for about 7 minutes.

3. Add the kale, cover, and cook for 7 to 10 minutes, or until the quinoa is cooked and the kale is tender. Remove from the heat.

4. Garnish with Hemp Heart "Parmesan" (if using).

Leftovers Tip: Leftovers of this dish are excellent served warm with a piece of toasted Quick Spelt Bread (page 136).

PER SERVING: Calories: 315; Fat: 3.7g; Dietary fiber: 8.4g; Protein: 16.3 g; Carbohydrates: 55.3g

SWEET POTATO AND CHICKPEA CURRY

SERVES 4 TO 6

PREP TIME: 5 MINUTES | COOK TIME: 25 MINUTES

This meal comes together with a delicate balance of spices. I prefer a simple blend of the ones seen here over a strong-flavored store-bought curry powder. Unsweetened nondairy yogurt offers a cool, tangy counterpoint when paired with this dish.

4 cups diced (½-inch) peeled
   sweet potato

2 cups vegetable broth

1 (15-ounce) can chickpeas, drained
   and rinsed

1 (10-ounce) bag frozen spinach

3 tablespoons tomato paste

1 tablespoon ground cumin

2 teaspoons ground coriander

1 teaspoon ground turmeric

1 teaspoon ground ginger

1 teaspoon garlic powder

½ teaspoon red pepper flakes

2 cups cooked brown rice

1. In a Dutch oven or saucepan, combine the sweet potato, broth, chickpeas, spinach, tomato paste, cumin, coriander, turmeric, ginger, garlic powder, and red pepper flakes. Bring to a boil over high heat.

2. Reduce the heat to low. Cover, and simmer for 20 minutes, or until the sweet potato is tender and a knife slides in easily. Remove from the heat.

3. Serve the curry over the brown rice.

PER SERVING: Calories: 293; Fat: 6g; Dietary fiber: 3.5g; Protein: 5.6g; Carbohydrates: 56.7g

Tiramisu, page 120

CHAPTER 7

DESSERTS

SWEET POTATO AND CHOCOLATE PUDDING

SERVES 4

PREP TIME: 10 MINUTES

Creamy chocolate pudding was a popular treat in my household when I was growing up. My mom would make fancy little cups for us to enjoy as dessert. I love this WFPB-based version because the texture is creamy and the flavor is rich and dark chocolatey.

2 cups cooked sweet potato, cooled

1 cup pitted dates

¾ cup unsweetened soy milk

6 tablespoons cocoa powder

1½ teaspoons vanilla extract

In a high-efficiency blender, combine the sweet potato, dates, soy milk, cocoa powder, and vanilla. Blend until smooth, using a tamper accessory if necessary. Refrigerate in an airtight container until ready to serve.

Ingredient Tip: If the dates are hard, simply microwave them on high for 20 seconds to soften them.

PER SERVING: Calories: 263; Fat: 2.2g; Dietary fiber: 9.6g; Protein: 6.1g; Carbohydrates: 61.6g

CHOCOLATE CHIP OAT COOKIES

MAKES 20 COOKIES

PREP TIME: 10 MINUTES | COOK TIME: 15 MINUTES

It's a win-win with these treats, which have the sweet taste of a decadent cookie (thanks to the tahini) and pack the nutritional punch of a granola bar (thanks to the oats, hemp hearts, and almond butter).

¾ cup oat flour

¾ cup rolled oats

2 tablespoons hemp hearts or chia seeds

¼ cup pure maple syrup

3 tablespoons unsalted, unsweetened almond butter or other nut butter

2 tablespoons tahini

1 tablespoon unsweetened soy milk

1 teaspoon vanilla extract

¼ cup vegan mini chocolate chips

1. Preheat the oven to 350°F. Line a baking sheet with parchment paper.

2. In a large bowl, mix together the flour, oats, and hemp hearts.

3. Add the maple syrup, almond butter, tahini, soy milk, and vanilla. Mix thoroughly.

4. Stir in the chocolate chips.

5. Drop 20 (1-tablespoon) dough balls, evenly spaced, onto the prepared baking sheet, and gently press down to create flat cookies.

6. Transfer the baking sheet to the oven, and bake for 12 minutes, or until the edges are golden brown. Remove from the oven. Let the cookies cool on the baking sheet for 10 minutes, then move to a wire rack to cool completely. Store in an airtight container.

PER SERVING (1 COOKIE): Calories: 151; Fat: 8.2g; Dietary fiber: 2.6g; Protein: 4.7g; Carbohydrates: 16.1g

MOLASSES-GINGER OAT COOKIE BALLS

MAKES 1 DOZEN COOKIES
PREP TIME: 10 MINUTES | COOK TIME: 15 MINUTES

The by-product of refining sugar cane, blackstrap molasses packs a nutritional punch. It's high in iron, calcium, magnesium, and selenium, but even though it's sweet, its rich and deep flavor can be too intense for some. In these cookies, the flavors of dates, ginger, and vanilla help balance it out. The nutritional benefits of blackstrap molasses far outweigh those of regular molasses, so be sure you are buying blackstrap.

1 cup pitted dates

3 tablespoons unsalted, unsweetened almond butter

2 tablespoons blackstrap molasses

1 teaspoon vanilla extract

1 cup oat flour

¼ cup rolled oats

½ teaspoon baking powder

1 teaspoon ground ginger

½ teaspoon ground cinnamon

⅛ teaspoon ground nutmeg

⅛ teaspoon ground cardamom

1. Preheat the oven to 350°F. Line a baking sheet with parchment paper.

2. In a food processor, combine the dates and almond butter. Blend to a creamy paste. Transfer to a large bowl.

3. Stir in the molasses and vanilla.

4. In a medium bowl, thoroughly combine the flour, oats, baking powder, ginger, cinnamon, nutmeg, and cardamom.

5. Fold the flour mixture into the molasses mixture.

6. Drop 12 (1-tablespoon) dough balls about 1 inch apart onto the prepared baking sheet.

7. Bake for 12 to 15 minutes, or until the edges are golden brown and the cookie balls are slightly firm to the touch. Remove from the oven.

Ingredient Tip: If you'd rather make your own oat flour, simply process rolled oats in a high-efficiency blender or food processor until the texture is flour-like. I process a whole canister at a time to have on hand in my pantry.

PER SERVING (1 COOKIE BALL): Calories: 275; Fat: 9.9g; Dietary fiber: 5.9g; Protein: 6.2g; Carbohydrates: 44.3g

PEANUT BUTTER OAT COOKIES

MAKES 24 COOKIES

PREP TIME: 10 MINUTES | COOK TIME: 15 MINUTES

A warm peanut butter cookie right from the oven is one of my all-time favorites, but traditional peanut butter cookies are laden with butter or oil. This WFPB version, made with applesauce and maple syrup, is just as tasty and moist and even has the requisite fork marks on top.

1 cup oat flour

½ cup rolled oats

¼ cup chopped roasted, unsalted peanuts

½ cup unsweetened natural peanut butter

5 tablespoons unsweetened applesauce

3 tablespoons pure maple syrup

1. Preheat the oven to 350°F. Line a baking sheet with parchment paper.

2. In a large bowl, mix together the flour, oats, and peanuts.

3. Add the peanut butter, applesauce, and maple syrup. Mix thoroughly.

4. Drop 24 (1-tablespoon) dough balls, evenly spaced, onto the prepared baking sheet. Using a fork (dip your fork in applesauce to keep it from sticking in the cookie), gently press down to create ridges.

5. Bake for 10 to 12 minutes, or until the edges are golden brown. Remove from the oven. Let the cookies cool on the baking sheet. Store in an airtight container.

PER SERVING (1 COOKIE): Calories: 69; Fat: 3.8g; Dietary fiber: 1g; Protein: 2.5g; Carbohydrates: 7g

APPLE-OAT CRISP

SERVES 4 TO 6

PREP TIME: 5 MINUTES | COOK TIME: 25 MINUTES

Many fruit crisps use butter, but the applesauce used in this recipe adds a nice texture and moisture while still creating a golden-brown biscuit-style topping. Granny Smith apples retain a slightly crisp texture when baked, so I recommend using those or another firm, crisp apple. Top with Nice Cream (page 116) if you like.

4 medium Granny Smith apples, cored and cut into ½-inch-thick slices

¾ cup pure maple syrup, divided

1 tablespoon lemon juice

½ teaspoon ground cinnamon

⅛ teaspoon ground nutmeg

¼ teaspoon tapioca starch

⅔ cup rolled oats

⅔ cup oat flour

⅓ cup unsweetened applesauce

1. Preheat the oven to 350°F.

2. In a medium bowl, mix together the apples, ½ cup of maple syrup, the lemon juice, cinnamon, nutmeg, and tapioca starch until the apples are well coated.

3. Spread the apples out in a single layer in an 8-by-8-inch glass baking dish or a 9-inch pie plate.

4. In a medium bowl, mix together the oats, oat flour, remaining ¼ cup of maple syrup, and the applesauce until well combined. Scoop the oat mixture in dollops onto the apples, and spread gently, trying to cover all the apples.

5. Transfer the baking dish to the oven, and bake for 20 to 25 minutes, or until the oat mixture is golden brown. Remove from the oven.

PER SERVING: Calories: 344; Fat: 2.5g; Dietary fiber: 8.7g; Protein: 4.5g; Carbohydrates: 80.3g

CARAMEL-COCONUT FROSTED BROWNIES

MAKES 12 BROWNIES

PREP TIME: 5 MINUTES | COOK TIME: 25 MINUTES

German chocolate cake is the inspiration for this recipe. The rich, decadent chocolate brownie paired with the gooey caramel-coconut frosting makes for a delicious and satisfying sweet treat that also happens to be WFPB approved. You won't even notice these brownies are made from beans.

For the brownies

1 (15-ounce) can black beans, drained and rinsed

½ cup rolled oats

6 tablespoons pure maple syrup

⅓ cup cocoa powder

⅓ cup unsweetened applesauce

2 tablespoons unsalted, unsweetened almond butter

1 teaspoon vanilla extract

Pinch ground cinnamon

For the frosting

1 cup pitted dates

6 tablespoons unsweetened plant-based milk

2 tablespoons nutritional yeast

¼ teaspoon vanilla extract

⅛ teaspoon red miso paste

¼ cup chopped pecans

3 tablespoons unsweetened coconut flakes

To make the brownies

1. Preheat the oven to 350°F. Line a 12-cup cupcake tin with liners.

2. In a food processor, combine the beans, oats, maple syrup, cocoa powder, applesauce, almond butter, vanilla, and cinnamon. Process until smooth.

3. Transfer the mixture to the prepared cupcake tin, about 2 tablespoons per cup to start, then evenly divide the remaining mixture.

4. Bake for 20 to 22 minutes, or until the tops are crispy and a toothpick inserted into the center of a cupcake comes out mostly clean. Remove from the oven. Remove the brownies from the tin, and transfer to a wire rack to cool for about 5 minutes.

5. Meanwhile, in a food processor, combine the dates, milk, nutritional yeast, vanilla, and miso. Process until mostly smooth.

6. Pulse in the pecans and coconut until well mixed but with some texture remaining.

7. Add 1 heaping tablespoon of the frosting per brownie, and serve.

Ingredient Tip: If the dates are hard, simply microwave them on high for 20 seconds to soften them.

PER SERVING (1 BROWNIE): Calories: 235; Fat: 11g; Dietary fiber: 12.4g; Protein: 9.8g; Carbohydrates: 30.4g

YOGURT PARFAIT 2 WAYS

SERVES 2

PREP TIME: 15 MINUTES

These creamy, tangy layered yogurt cups are ready in minutes. I like to use Kite Hill unsweetened yogurt because it has the least number of ingredients, but any unsweetened nondairy yogurt will work. Tahini adds a depth of flavor and also thickens the yogurt to a more pudding-like texture, which makes layering the dessert easier.

VANILLA YOGURT AND BERRY CUP

1 cup nondairy vegan yogurt

2 tablespoons pure maple syrup

2 tablespoons tahini

½ teaspoon vanilla extract

½ cup Tahini-Maple Granola
(page 128)

½ cup blueberries

½ cup diced strawberries

1. In a medium bowl, mix together the yogurt, maple syrup, tahini, and vanilla.

2. In a small serving dish, layer ¼ cup of granola, ¼ cup of yogurt mixture, ¼ cup of blueberries, and ¼ cup of strawberries. Repeat with a second layer of each. Refrigerate until ready to serve.

PER SERVING: Calories: 278; Fat: 16.5g; Dietary fiber: 3g; Protein: 6.9g; Carbohydrates: 24.9g

CHOCOLATE DIRT YOGURT CUP

¼ cup vegan chocolate chips

3 tablespoons sliced almonds

3 teaspoons cocoa powder, divided

2 teaspoons pure maple syrup, plus
2 tablespoons, divided

1 cup nondairy vegan yogurt

2 tablespoons tahini

½ teaspoon vanilla extract

½ cup blueberries

1. In a food processor, combine the chocolate chips, almonds, 2 teaspoons of cocoa powder, and 2 teaspoons of maple syrup. Process until crumbly, like dirt.

2. In a medium bowl, mix together the yogurt, remaining 2 tablespoons of maple syrup, the tahini, vanilla, and remaining 1 teaspoon of cocoa powder.

3. In a small serving dish, layer 1 tablespoon of the chocolate "dirt" mixture, ¼ cup of blueberries, and a layer of chocolate yogurt. Repeat with a second layer, and top with the remaining "dirt mixture." Refrigerate until ready to serve.

Variation Tip: Experiment with any berries you like or even stone fruit like cherries.

PER SERVING: Calories: 299; Fat: 17.2g; Dietary fiber: 5.8g; Protein: 14.6g; Carbohydrates: 49.6g

BLUEBERRY-LIME SORBET

SERVES 6
PREP TIME: 5 MINUTES

This is an added-sugar-free treat that will satisfy your sweet-tooth cravings. Raisins give this sorbet a grown-up subtle wine flavor, and the lime adds a brightness and balance. Fresh and frozen blueberries enhance the flavor and texture. Many sorbet recipes call for the addition of liquid, but I didn't want to dilute the flavor with water or add fat from a plant-based milk, and this recipe really doesn't need it—it's perfectly lip smacking as is.

1 cup frozen blueberries

1 cup fresh blueberries

3 to 6 ice cubes

¼ cup unsweetened raisins

2 tablespoons lime juice

In a high-efficiency blender, combine the frozen blueberries, fresh blueberries, ice, raisins, and lime juice. Blend for about 30 seconds, or until smooth. (You may need to use the tamping tool to move frozen ingredients toward the blades.) Serve immediately.

PER SERVING: Calories: 116; Fat: 0.6g; Dietary fiber: 3.9g; Protein: 1.5g; Carbohydrates: 30g

MILK SHAKES WITH CHOCOLATE SAUCE

SERVES 2

PREP TIME: 10 MINUTES

Inspired by diner-style milk shakes, this recipe uses frozen bananas to achieve a thick, creamy texture and amps up the sweet flavor with dates and vanilla. These shakes are crave-worthy enough on their own, but a final drizzle of chocolate sauce puts them over-the-top. Note that if your dates are hard, you can microwave them for 20 seconds to soften.

For the chocolate sauce

¾ cup unsweetened soy milk
½ cup pitted dates
2 tablespoons cocoa powder

For the shakes

4 frozen bananas
1 cup unsweetened soy milk
4 pitted dates (about ¼ cup)
2 teaspoons vanilla extract

To make the chocolate sauce

1. In a high-efficiency blender, combine the soy milk, dates, and cocoa powder. Blend for 30 seconds, or until smooth. Transfer to a bowl. Clean the blender.

To make the shakes

2. In the blender, combine the bananas, soy milk, dates, and vanilla. Blend for 30 seconds, or until smooth. Divide between 2 serving glasses.

3. Drizzle with the chocolate sauce. Serve immediately.

Variation Tip: For a strawberry shake, add ¼ to ½ cup fresh or frozen and thawed strawberries to the blender when you add the bananas.

PER SERVING: Calories: 538; Fat: 5.5g; Dietary fiber: 14.4g; Protein: 12.2g; Carbohydrates: 120.9g

NICE CREAM

SERVES 2

PREP TIME: 10 MINUTES

There is no wrong way to enjoy nice cream, the perfect frozen indulgence whether it's on a hot summer day or you're cozied up on the couch in front of the fire. The key to this recipe is the frozen bananas. I've been known to buy bananas simply to freeze them for nice cream. You want to freeze them when they start to get brown and spotty so they are sweet, but not mushy. To freeze, simply peel, break into four or five chunks, put in a freezer-safe plastic zip-top bag, squeeze out the air, seal the bag, and lay flat in a single layer in your freezer. It typically takes at least six hours to freeze solid and be ready for nice cream.

2 cups frozen banana chunks
1 tablespoon soy milk
½ teaspoon vanilla extract

1. In a food processor, process the bananas until crumbly.

2. Add the soy milk and vanilla. Process until the ingredients begin to form a ball and resemble soft-serve ice cream. Serve immediately.

Variation Tip: To flavor your nice cream, when adding the soy milk you can add one of these variations: 1 cup frozen strawberries, 2 tablespoons peanut butter, or 2 tablespoons cocoa powder.

PER SERVING: Calories: 112; Fat: 0.5g; Dietary fiber: 3.1g; Protein: 1.5g; Carbohydrates: 27.6g

ZABAGLIONE CASHEW CREAM

SERVES 4

PREP TIME: 5 MINUTES

Inspired by the Italian dessert zabaglione, egg yolks blended with wine and sugar, I made this easy and delicious sweet cashew cream. Raisins contribute a subtle grape flavor in place of the wine. Look for organic 100 percent apple juice with no added sugars or preservatives. I like to serve this dessert in a fancy glass or cup over berries or peaches, drizzled over Poached Pears (page 118), or as a dip for sliced fruit.

½ cup raw cashews

½ cup apple juice

½ cup unsweetened raisins

2 teaspoons lemon juice

Fresh berries or other fruits, for serving

1. In a high-efficiency blender, combine the cashews, apple juice, raisins, and lemon juice. Blend until smooth. Transfer to an airtight container, and refrigerate until ready to serve.

2. To serve, put fruit in a bowl or dessert dish, and drizzle with the zabaglione.

PER SERVING: Calories: 231; Fat: 8g; Dietary fiber: 2.5g; Protein: 2.9g; Carbohydrates: 39.8g

POACHED PEARS

SERVES 2 TO 4

PREP TIME: 10 MINUTES | COOK TIME: 20 MINUTES

Selecting the right pears for this fancy-but-fast dish is key, since the firmer and less ripe the pears are, the longer they take to cook. I find slightly ripe pears to be perfect, yielding a nice sweet and soft texture when poached. I use Bosc pears due to their dense flesh. To identify a perfectly ripe pear, press gently on the top near the stem; it should have a slight give.

2 cups apple juice

¼ cup unsweetened raisins

½ teaspoon ground cinnamon

½ teaspoon vanilla extract

4 to 6 slightly ripe Bosc pears, peeled

Zabaglione Cashew Cream (page 117), for serving (optional)

1. In a large pan with a flat bottom, combine the apple juice, raisins, cinnamon, and vanilla. Place over high heat.

2. Quarter the pears. Using a melon baller, scoop out the seeds (or trim them out with a paring knife).

3. Add the pears to the liquid. Bring to a boil. Reduce the heat to medium. Partially cover, and simmer for 20 minutes, or until the pears are tender (a paring knife should easily slide into the pears). Remove from the heat.

4. Serve the poached pears with a drizzle of the cooking liquid or a drizzle of zabaglione (if using).

PER SERVING: Calories: 343; Fat: 1.9g; Dietary fiber: 3.7g; Protein: 0.3g; Carbohydrates: 89g

PUMPKIN SPICE RICE PUDDING

SERVES 8

PREP TIME: 5 MINUTES | COOK TIME: 20 MINUTES

Pumpkin spice gives me all the warm and cozy autumn feels. This spiced rice pudding uses whole-food ingredients to create a delightful cold-weather comfort dessert. I also find that it's an excellent way to use up leftover brown rice. Starting with pumpkin puree, not pumpkin pie filling, allows you to control the ingredients, since many of the pumpkin pie mixes contain sugar. This pudding may be served warm or chilled.

3 cups cooked brown rice

1 (15½-ounce) can unsweetened
    coconut milk

1 (15½-ounce) can pumpkin puree

6 tablespoons pure maple syrup

1 tablespoon vanilla extract

1 teaspoon ground cinnamon

1 teaspoon ground ginger

½ teaspoon ground nutmeg

¼ teaspoon ground cloves

1 teaspoon lemon juice

Tahini-Maple Granola (page 128),
    for serving

Unsweetened raisins, for serving

1. In a medium saucepan, combine the rice, coconut milk, pumpkin puree, maple syrup, vanilla, cinnamon, ginger, nutmeg, and cloves. Bring to a boil over high heat.

2. Reduce the heat to medium-low. Simmer for 20 minutes, or until the rice mixture takes on a thick pudding-like consistency. Remove from the heat.

3. Stir in the lemon juice.

4. Serve the pudding warm or chilled with granola and raisins.

PER SERVING: Calories: 423; Fat: 15.2g; Dietary fiber: 5.5g; Protein: 7.3g; Carbohydrates: 65.8g

TIRAMISU

SERVES 6 TO 8

PREP TIME: 20 MINUTES | COOK TIME: 10 MINUTES

One of my favorite desserts of all time is tiramisu. I love the balanced flavors of the strong coffee and the rich cream. To achieve a WFPB version, I use whole-grain bread instead of the traditional cookies, soaked in sweet, strong coffee. Cashew cream provides a nice texture and mild flavor, a perfect complement to the coffee-soaked bread. Toasting the bread prior to soaking allows it to retain its shape.

9 Quick Spelt Bread (page 136) or whole-grain bread slices, crusts removed

½ cup strong coffee or espresso, chilled

2 tablespoons pure maple syrup, divided

⅛ teaspoon almond extract

1 cup raw cashews

½ cup unsweetened soy milk

¼ cup pitted dates

1 tablespoon lemon juice

Cocoa powder, for dusting

1. Line a baking sheet with parchment paper.

2. Arrange the bread in a single layer on the prepared baking sheet.

3. Transfer the baking sheet to a cold oven, and heat to 350°F.

4. When the oven reaches temperature, flip the bread over, and toast for another 5 to 7 minutes. Remove from the oven.

5. Meanwhile, in a shallow bowl, mix together the coffee, 1 tablespoon of maple syrup, and the almond extract.

6. To make the cashew cream, combine the cashews, soy milk, dates, remaining 1 tablespoon of maple syrup, and the lemon juice in a high-efficiency blender. Process until smooth.

7. Once cool enough to handle, dip the toasted bread in the coffee mixture.

8. In an 8-by-8-inch glass baking dish, layer the bread followed by half of the cashew cream. Repeat with a second layer. Cover, and refrigerate until ready to serve.

9. Slice the tiramisu, sift cocoa powder on top, and serve

Variation Tip: I have also served this with a drizzle of homemade chocolate sauce (see page 115) for extra decadence.

PER SERVING: Calories: 301; Fat: 11.8g; Dietary fiber: 5.9g; Protein: 10.4g; Carbohydrates: 41.3g

Tahini-Maple Granola, page 128

CHAPTER 8

STAPLES

ALL-PURPOSE SPICE BLENDS

PREP TIME: 5 MINUTES

Having a couple of homemade spice blends on hand to add to meals will help you avoid store-bought versions, many of which contain a lot of salt. These two provide a robust flavor and make it even easier to prepare the recipes in the book. You can also use them to season just about any dish at the table. The chili blend works well sprinkled on tropical fruits, like pineapple and mango, with a squeeze of lime, too.

ITALIAN SEASONING

MAKES 9 TABLESPOONS

8 teaspoons dried marjoram

8 teaspoons dried basil

4 teaspoons dried thyme

2 teaspoons dried rosemary

2 teaspoons dried sage

2 teaspoons dried oregano

1 teaspoon garlic powder

In an airtight container with a lid (or repurposed spice jar), combine the marjoram, basil, thyme, rosemary, sage, oregano, and garlic powder. Shake or mix well.

CHILI SPICE BLEND

MAKES 7½ TABLESPOONS

¼ cup chili powder

4 teaspoons onion powder

4 teaspoons ground cumin

1 teaspoon ground coriander

1 teaspoon garlic powder

½ teaspoon cayenne

In an airtight container with a lid (or repurposed spice jar), combine the chili powder, onion powder, cumin, coriander, garlic powder, and cayenne. Shake or mix well.

Pair It With: The Chili Spice Blend always goes well with a squeeze of zesty lime juice, as in the Baja-Style Tacos (page 64).

HEMP HEART "PARMESAN"

MAKES ABOUT 1 CUP
PREP TIME: 5 MINUTES

This nutty and "cheesy" ingredient is a perfect substitute for Parmesan cheese, which was something I did miss early in my plant-based transition. I love the simplicity of this parmesan, using hemp hearts and mixing (versus getting out my food processor). The texture of the hemp hearts gives the parmesan a nice hearty bite, while nutritional yeast adds umami. Hemp hearts provide a nice serving of omega-3 and omega-6 fatty acids, which help promote brain health. Use this wherever you might have sprinkles of parmesan. I like it on my WFPB pizzas and pasta dishes.

½ cup plus 2 tablespoons hemp hearts

½ cup nutritional yeast

¼ teaspoon garlic powder

In a small container with a lid, combine the hemp hearts, nutritional yeast, and garlic powder. Shake or stir. Store in the refrigerator for up to 1 month.

PER SERVING (2 TEASPOONS): Calories: 54; Fat: 3.4g; Dietary fiber: 1.6g; Protein: 4g; Carbohydrates: 2.3g

HOMEMADE BARBECUE SAUCE & KETCHUP

MAKES ABOUT 2 CUPS OF BARBECUE SAUCE OR 3 CUPS OF KETCHUP
PREP TIME: 10 MINUTES

Homemade condiments generally just taste better than store-bought ones, and you can control your ingredients. I used different sweeteners in each of these based on the flavor I'm trying to achieve. Use them wherever you would typically add these condiments. I like to top my Black Bean Burgers (page 66) with the barbecue sauce for a Western-style burger or use it on grilled vegetables and tofu for a hearty barbecue dish.

BARBECUE SAUCE

1 (8-ounce) can tomato sauce

3 pitted dates

¼ cup apple cider vinegar

3 tablespoons blackstrap molasses

2 tablespoons whole-grain mustard

1½ teaspoons onion powder

1½ teaspoons smoked paprika

½ teaspoon garlic powder

⅛ teaspoon cayenne

In a high-efficiency blender or food processor, combine the tomato sauce, dates, vinegar, molasses, mustard, onion powder, paprika, garlic powder, and cayenne. Process until smooth. Store leftovers in an airtight container in the refrigerator for up to 1 week.

PER SERVING (2 TABLESPOONS): Calories: 45; Fat: 0.3g; Dietary fiber: 0.9g; Protein: 0.6g; Carbohydrates: 10.5g

KETCHUP

1 (15-ounce) can tomato sauce

1 cup unsweetened raisins

½ cup distilled white vinegar

2 teaspoons onion powder

½ teaspoon garlic powder

¼ teaspoon ground coriander

In a high-efficiency blender or food processor, combine the tomato sauce, raisins, vinegar, onion powder, garlic powder, and coriander. Process until smooth. Store leftovers in an airtight container in the refrigerator for up to 1 week.

Variation Tip: You can halve the ketchup recipe by starting with 1 (8-ounce) can tomato sauce and reducing all the other ingredients by half. You can also make a spicy version by adding cayenne to taste.

PER SERVING (2 TABLESPOONS): Calories: 35; Fat: 0.1g; Dietary fiber: 1.1g; Protein: 0.9g; Carbohydrates: 7.5g

TAHINI-MAPLE GRANOLA

MAKES ABOUT 2½ CUPS
PREP TIME: 10 MINUTES | COOK TIME: 40 MINUTES

This recipe was inspired by the tahini bars made by Mighty Sesame (my preferred brand of tahini due to taste, texture, and viscosity). You can enjoy this granola as a breakfast topper, as a snack, or in a bowl with fresh fruit and plant-based milk.

1 cup rolled oats
¼ cup unsweetened raisins
¼ cup pecan pieces
¼ cup walnut pieces
¼ cup sliced almonds
¼ cup vegan chocolate chips
3 tablespoons tahini
3 tablespoons pure maple syrup

1. Preheat the oven to 350°F. Line a baking sheet with parchment paper.

2. In a large bowl, combine the oats, raisins, pecans, walnuts, almonds, and chocolate chips.

3. Add the tahini and maple syrup. Mix thoroughly.

4. Spread the mixture out in a thin layer on the prepared baking sheet (for a chunkier granola, leave small chunks together).

5. Transfer the baking sheet to the oven, and bake for 35 to 40 minutes, stirring halfway through, or until the granola is crispy and golden brown. Remove from the oven. Store in an airtight container for up to 1 week.

PER SERVING (¼ CUP): Calories: 145; Fat: 7.8g; Dietary fiber: 2.1g; Protein: 3.6g; Carbohydrates: 1.8g

TOFU "RICOTTA"

MAKES ABOUT 2½ CUPS
PREP TIME: 10 MINUTES

Firm tofu provides a creamy and textured base for this take on ricotta cheese, and it is a great staple to have on hand that you can make savory (as outlined in the method) or sweet, depending on your application. Use this in a WFPB lasagna or to top your WFPB pizza.

7 ounces firm tofu, drained

2 tablespoons Hemp Heart "Parmesan" (page 125)

1 teaspoon lemon juice

In a small bowl with a lid, using a fork, mash the tofu, parmesan, and lemon juice. Store covered in the refrigerator for up to 5 days.

Variation Tip: Sweeten it up with a little lemon and maple syrup, and use it in dessert recipes or serve over fresh fruit.

PER SERVING (¼ CUP): Calories: 34; Fat: 2.4g; Dietary fiber: 0.5g; Protein: 2.9g; Carbohydrates: 0.7g

FRUIT-CHIA JAM

MAKES ABOUT 1 CUP

PREP TIME: 5 MINUTES | COOK TIME: 10 MINUTES

Yes, it's possible to make a sweet and thick fruit jam without all the sugar. Using raisins provides a sweet, slightly grape-like flavor. Chia seeds thicken the jam and pack a nice hearty boost of healthy omega-3 and omega-6 fatty acids as well as iron. These jams are a refrigerator staple that will help brighten your morning toast or bowl of oats, or you can drizzle them over a dessert.

BLUEBERRY-CHIA JAM

1 cup fresh or thawed frozen blueberries

¼ cup unsweetened raisins

¼ cup water

1 tablespoon chia seeds

1. In a small saucepan, combine the blueberries, raisins, and water. Cook over medium heat, mashing with a fork or potato masher, for about 5 minutes, or until thickened.

2. Reduce the heat to medium-low. Stir in the chia seeds, and continue to mash as the jam thickens slightly. Remove from the heat. Store in an airtight container in the refrigerator for up to 1 week. The jam will thicken in the refrigerator.

PER SERVING (2 TABLESPOONS): Calories: 29; Fat: 0.6g; Dietary fiber: 1.4g; Protein: 0.6g; Carbohydrates: 6.2g

STRAWBERRY-CHIA JAM

1 cup fresh or thawed frozen
    strawberries

¼ cup chopped pitted dates

½ cup water

1 tablespoon chia seeds

1. In a small saucepan, combine the strawberries, dates, and water. Cook over medium heat, mashing with a fork or potato masher, for about 5 minutes, or until thickened.

2. Reduce the heat to medium-low. Stir in the chia seeds, and continue to mash as the jam thickens slightly. Remove from the heat. Store in an airtight container in the refrigerator for up to 1 week. The jam will thicken in the refrigerator.

BLUEBERRY PER SERVING (2 TABLESPOONS): Calories: 31; Fat: 0.6g; Dietary fiber: 1.2g; Protein: 0.7g; Carbohydrates: 6.9g

SMOKY MUSHROOMS

MAKES 2 CUPS

PREP TIME: 10 MINUTES | COOK TIME: 10 MINUTES

A smoky, savory ingredient for sandwiches, pastas, and more, these mushrooms are a versatile flavor booster. Bursting with a sweet and smoky bacon-like taste and rich umami, these mushrooms are sure to make your mouth water. Use these to top a cheesy macaroni dish, or add them to your next plant-based breakfast sandwich for some baconesque goodness.

2 tablespoons soy sauce

2 tablespoons pure maple syrup

1 tablespoon liquid smoke

1 tablespoon liquid aminos

¼ teaspoon freshly ground black pepper

1 pound cremini mushrooms, cut into ½-inch-thick slices

1. In a sauté pan or skillet, whisk together the soy sauce, maple syrup, liquid smoke, liquid aminos, and pepper.

2. Add the mushrooms, and cook over medium-high heat, stirring frequently, for about 10 minutes, or until the liquid evaporates but the mushrooms are still tender and glistening. Remove from the heat. Store in an airtight container in the refrigerator until ready to use.

PER SERVING (½ CUP): Calories: 45; Fat: 0.1g; Dietary fiber: 0.8g; Protein: 3.3g; Carbohydrates: 8.4g

HOMEMADE BEANS

MAKES ABOUT 3 CUPS

PREP TIME: 5 MINUTES | COOK TIME: 2 TO 3 HOURS

Beans are a staple in my house, and I recommend them for anyone following a whole-food, plant-based diet. I love cooking dried beans this way and have tried it with every type of bean. The addition of the kelp granules aids digestion and softens the beans' exterior to allow for a creamier texture that works in any recipe. Simply use 1½ cups of these homemade beans wherever you would use canned beans. Yum!

8 ounces dried beans, picked over and rinsed

3½ cups water

Pinch kelp granules

1. In a Dutch oven or saucepan, combine the beans, water, and kelp. Bring to a boil over high heat.

2. Reduce the heat to low. Cover, and simmer for the cooking time noted in the bean cooking chart. Remove from the heat.

BEAN COOKING CHART

I recommend tasting your beans to be sure they are tender and creamy at the time noted in the table. Add half-hour increments until they reach your desired texture.

TYPE OF DRIED BEAN	COOKING TIME	PER SERVING (¼ CUP)
Chickpeas	2½ hours	Calories: 120; Fat: 2g; Dietary fiber: 12g; Protein: 9g; Carbohydrates: 28g
Black beans	1½ hours	Calories: 110; Fat: 0.5g; Dietary fiber: 16g; Protein: 11g; Carbohydrates: 29g
White beans	2 hours	Calories: 120; Fat: 0.5g; Dietary fiber: 12g; Protein: 9g; Carbohydrates: 28g
Pinto beans	2 hours	Calories: 110; Fat: 0.5g; Dietary fiber: 11g; Protein: 8g; Carbohydrates: 26g

PERFECT BAKED TOFU

SERVES 8

PREP TIME: 5 MINUTES | COOK TIME: 40 MINUTES

These baked tofu slabs have a perfect texture and will take on the flavor of any dish you are adding them to. I love to chill, chop, and mix these with a WFPB-friendly mayo, mustard, minced vegetables, and spices to make an egg-style salad; add to a toasted whole-grain bun with Homemade Barbecue Sauce (page 126); or use in place of a fried egg in breakfast sandwiches.

2 (14-ounce) packages firm
    tofu, drained
Freshly ground black pepper

1. Preheat the oven to 450°F.

2. Cut each package of tofu into 8 equal slabs about ½ inch thick.

3. Arrange the tofu in a single layer on a parchment-lined baking sheet. Season with pepper.

4. Bake for 20 minutes, or until the tofu is starting to dry and slightly firm to the touch.

5. Carefully flip the tofu over. Season with pepper. Bake for 15 to 20 minutes, or until the tofu is dry and firm and the edges are slightly crispy. Remove from the oven. Store in an airtight container in the refrigerator until ready to use.

Variation Tip: For a more savory version, lightly brush the tofu with liquid aminos before seasoning with pepper.

PER SERVING: Calories: 69; Fat: 4.1g; Dietary fiber: 0.9g; Protein: 8.1g; Carbohydrates: 1.7g

POTATO WEDGES

SERVES 2 TO 4

PREP TIME: 10 MINUTES | COOK TIME: 40 MINUTES

Having perfectly crispy potato wedges as a side for sandwiches makes for a satisfyingly complete meal. I have also been known to whip up a batch of these as dinner paired with a salad or as a snack to dip in Guacamole (page 39) or Ketchup (page 127). Snack, side, or main, these are delicious any time.

3 or 4 medium red potatoes, cut into ½-inch wedges (about 1 pound)

1. Preheat the oven to 450°F. Line a baking sheet with parchment paper.

2. Spread the potatoes out in a single layer on the prepared baking sheet.

3. Bake for 15 to 20 minutes, or until the potatoes are browned and crispy.

4. Flip the potatoes over, and bake for 15 to 20 minutes, or until crispy. Remove from the oven. Serve immediately.

PER SERVING: Calories: 149; Fat: 0.3g; Dietary fiber: 3.6g; Protein: 4g; Carbohydrates: 33.9g

QUICK SPELT BREAD

MAKES 1 LOAF

PREP TIME: 5 MINUTES | COOK TIME: 45 MINUTES

Nothing beats the smell of homemade bread—especially when it doesn't take all day to make. Using ground whole-grain spelt flour instead of overprocessed white flour is not just healthier. It results in bread with a nuttier, deeper flavor. I like to dip my bread pieces in a rich balsamic vinegar mixed with Italian Seasoning (page 124).

420 grams whole-grain spelt flour
(about 3¾ cups)
1 teaspoon baking soda
1 teaspoon baking powder
1½ cups unsweetened soy milk
2 tablespoons pure maple syrup
1 tablespoon lemon juice

1. Preheat the oven to 350°F.

2. Cut parchment paper to evenly line a 9-by-5-inch loaf pan by cutting inward to make the corners fit snugly. Allow the parchment paper to pass the top of the loaf pan (you will use these to remove the loaf from the pan in step 7).

3. In a large bowl, mix together the flour, baking soda, and baking powder.

4. In a medium bowl, mix together the soy milk, maple syrup, and lemon juice.

5. Add the soy milk mixture to the flour mixture, and mix well until combined, all the flour has hydrated, gluten has started to form, and the dough gets a little harder to mix. Transfer to the prepared loaf pan.

6. Bake for 45 minutes, or until the loaf is golden brown and a wooden skewer inserted into the center comes out clean. Remove from the oven.

7. Using the parchment paper as a sling, remove the bread from the loaf pan, and let cool completely before cutting.

Pair It With: This bread is perfect for Tiramisu (page 120) and pairs very well with savory Romesco-Style Hummus (page 37).

PER SERVING (1 1-INCH SLICE): Calories: 204; Fat: 1.7g; Dietary fiber: 6.4g; Protein: 8.2g; Carbohydrates: 42.1g

PERFECT MARINARA SAUCE

MAKES 7 CUPS

PREP TIME: 10 MINUTES | COOK TIME: 20 MINUTES

This simple homemade marinara sauce using our homemade Italian Seasoning (page 124) is perfect for weeknight or weekend meals. It can be used as a pizza sauce or in any of your favorite pasta recipes. Another easy dinner option is to serve this sauce over a plate of farro, with a scoop of Tofu "Ricotta" (page 129) and broccoli or sautéed greens.

2 (28-ounce) cans crushed tomatoes in puree

4 garlic cloves, minced

2 tablespoons Italian Seasoning (page 124)

2 teaspoons pure maple syrup

2 teaspoons onion powder

2 teaspoons paprika

¼ teaspoon freshly ground black pepper

1. In a medium saucepan, stir together the tomatoes, garlic, Italian seasoning, maple syrup, onion powder, paprika, and pepper. Bring to a simmer.

2. Reduce the heat to low. Cover, and simmer for 15 to 20 minutes, or until the sauce is fragrant and the flavors have melded together. Remove from the heat.

Leftovers Tip: This sauce freezes and reheats well. I recommend freezing it in 1- or 2-cup batches to use in other recipes, like my Portabella Mushroom Sandwiches with Pesto "Ricotta" (page 68).

PER SERVING (⅓ CUP): Calories: 39; Fat: 0g; Dietary fiber: 1.9g; Protein: 1.9g; Carbohydrates: 7.8g

MEASUREMENT CONVERSIONS

Volume Equivalents	U.S. Standard	U.S. Standard (ounces)	Metric (approximate)
Liquid	2 tablespoons	1 fl. oz.	30 mL
	¼ cup	2 fl. oz.	60 mL
	½ cup	4 fl. oz.	120 mL
	1 cup	8 fl. oz.	240 mL
	1½ cups	12 fl. oz.	355 mL
	2 cups or 1 pint	16 fl. oz.	475 mL
	4 cups or 1 quart	32 fl. oz.	1 L
	1 gallon	128 fl. oz.	4 L
Dry	⅛ teaspoon	—	0.5 mL
	¼ teaspoon	—	1 mL
	½ teaspoon	—	2 mL
	¾ teaspoon	—	4 mL
	1 teaspoon	—	5 mL
	1 tablespoon	—	15 mL
	¼ cup	—	59 mL
	⅓ cup	—	79 mL
	½ cup	—	118 mL
	⅔ cup	—	156 mL
	¾ cup	—	177 mL
	1 cup	—	235 mL
	2 cups or 1 pint	—	475 mL
	3 cups	—	700 mL
	4 cups or 1 quart	—	1 L
	½ gallon	—	2 L
	1 gallon	—	4 L

Oven Temperatures

Fahrenheit	Celsius (approximate)
250°F	120°C
300°F	150°C
325°F	165°C
350°F	180°C
375°F	190°C
400°F	200°C
425°F	220°C
450°F	230°C

Weight Equivalents

U.S. Standard	Metric (approximate)
½ ounce	15 g
1 ounce	30 g
2 ounces	60 g
4 ounces	115 g
8 ounces	225 g
12 ounces	340 g
16 ounces or 1 pound	455 g

REFERENCES

Campbell, T. Colin. "Salt, Sugar, and Fat." *Center for Nutrition Studies*. July 6, 2020. NutritionStudies.org/salt-sugar-and-fat.

Esselstyn, Caldwell. "No Oil – Not Even Olive Oil!" Accessed August 3, 2020. YouTu.be/b_o4YBQPKtQ.

Greger, Michael. *How Not to Die: Discover the Foods Scientifically Proven to Prevent and Reverse Disease.* New York: Flatiron Books, 2015.

McDougall, John A. *The Starch Solution: Eat the Foods You Love, Regain Your Health, and Lose the Weight for Good!* New York: Rodale Inc., 2012.

McDougall, John A. "Vitamin D Supplements Are Harmful: Sunshine and Food Determine Health." *Dr. McDougall Health & Medical Center.* Accessed September 7, 2020. DrMcDougall.com/ 2015/03/31/vitamin-d-supplements-are-harmful-sunshine-and-food-determine-health.

Melina, Vesanto, Winston Craig, Susan Levin. "Position of the Academy of Nutrition and Dietetics: Vegetarian Diets." *Journal of the Academy of Nutrition and Dietetics* 116, no. 12 (December 2016): 1970–80. doi: 10.1016/j.jand.2016.09.025.

National Kidney Foundation. "Spice Up Your Diet without Salt." Accessed September 7, 2020. Kidney.org/news/kidneyCare/ spring10/WithoutSalt.

Williams, Kim A. "CardioBuzz: Vegan Diet, Healthy Heart?" *Med Page Today*. July 21, 2014. MedPageToday.com/Blogs/ CardioBuzz/46860.

INDEX

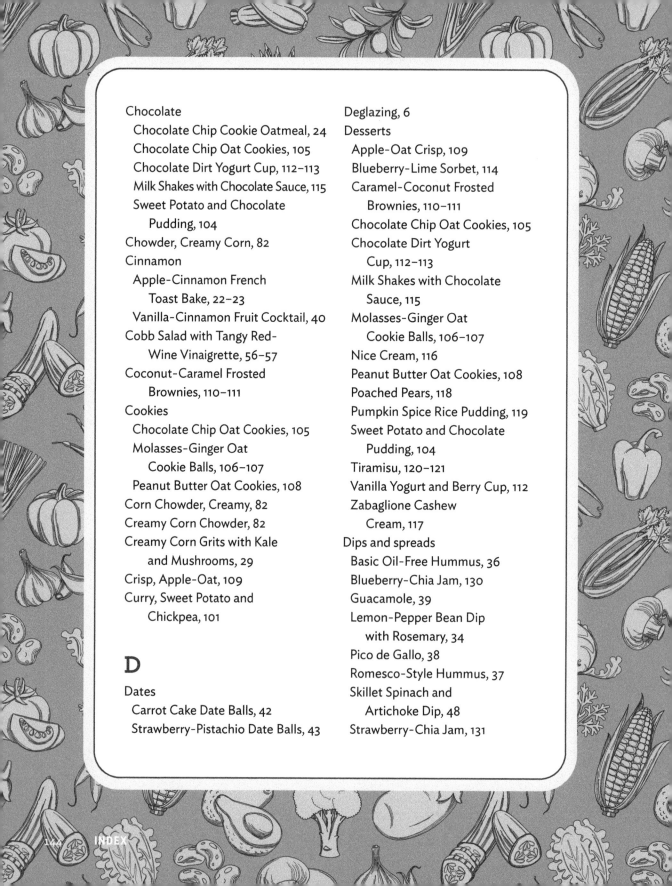

ACKNOWLEDGMENTS

First and foremost, thank you to the fans of VegInspired. You fuel my passion for sharing my knowledge about plant-based eating. Other thanks go to:

My husband, John, for your help throughout the recipe-development process. You are my best friend, and I am forever grateful for your belief in me. This cookbook would not be what it is without you.

My three cats, whose snuggles were a welcome distraction when I was deep in writing.

My parents, who tested recipes even though they don't follow a plant-based diet. I am grateful for all the meals we ate as a family growing up. Thank you for making that a priority.

My brother. I am so happy you could visit and get a sneak peek at one of my recipes.

My in-laws, whose home-cooked meals have always been an inspiration to me.

My awesome team of recipe testers: Marjorie Allen, Sarah Chapman, Aimee Douglass, Sherri Gibson, Patricia M., Marvin Retsky, Sue W., and many others.

Friends and family who checked in on my progress. You always brought a smile to my face.

The team at Callisto Media, who worked to make my dream of being a published cookbook author come true.

And to all the people like I was six years ago, transitioning to a plant-based diet. I hope these recipes inspire you to eat more plants.

ABOUT THE AUTHOR

Kathy A. Davis is a recipe developer, plant-based mentor, and educator. She has been creating and sharing delicious plant-based recipes with the world for more than six years. She is the co-founder of VegInspired, a plant-based lifestyle blog. Kathy has spoken at vegan events, and she and her recipes have been featured on One Green Planet and *Rootless Living Magazine*. Kathy is passionate about educating others about the health benefits of a plant-based lifestyle by creating and sharing simple and healthy recipes. With her husband, John, behind the camera, she guides people through some of their favorite recipes on her VegInspired YouTube channel.

Kathy has a master's degree in education from St. Bonaventure University. She attributes her passion for sharing knowledge with others to her continued desire for lifelong learning.

Kathy is currently traveling the United States in a fifth-wheel camper with her husband, John, and their three cats. Together they have a goal to visit all of the US national parks. When she is not cooking in their little RV kitchen, she can be found bicycling, hiking, or reading with a cat cozied up on her lap.

Connect with Kathy at www.veginspired.com or on Instagram (@veginspired); Facebook (www.facebook.com/Veginspired); Twitter (@veginspired); or YouTube (www.youtube.com/veginspired).